Dear Reader,

Savor this wonderful little book by a truly renaissance couple.

Their journey—as priest, nun, teachers, learners, inventors, entrepreneurs and parents—is one of unabashed passion, rich inspiration, and abundant creativity. They display a mix of skills any Medici would be honored to champion.

The genius of Maria and Charlie is their ability to wrap their arms around and simplify the many principles of creativity that it took me years to uncover during my own storied career. Espouse their tools and techniques and you will be the better for it. Those who have seen them train, facilitate, and motivate people in all walks of life already know of what I speak.

Prepare your soul for a refreshing plunge into the world of What If-What Else-Why Not! And finally, celebrate with me in the enlightenment that comes when creatives such as these are willing to share their wisdom and experience.

May this become the sketchbook in which you draw yourself creative!

Leonardo

Leonardo da Vinci
Florence, Italy
Summer Solstice, 2001

Published by:
Creativity Central
www.creativitycentral.com

Printed in the Unites States of America
Copyright © Charlie & Maria Girsch, 1999, 2005
All rights reserved
Illustrations by Dean Stanton

ISBN# 0-9676503-6-4
Library of Congress Control Number is 2001 117790
First printing, September 1999
Second printing, December 1999
Third printing, June 2000
Fourth printing, November 2000
Fifth printing, June 2001

Second edition, September 2001
Third edition, March 2003
Fourth edition, September 2005

Fanning the Creative Spirit

(formerly Inventivity)

by
Maria Girsch, Phn.D. & Charlie Girsch, Phn.D.

This book is
dedicated to
our six most wonderful inventions
chris, jon, tim, cat, geoff & charles

who reflect
each in his or her way

the
everyday creativity
of which we speak.

Kudos

Special thanks to
Ginny Moran, Steve Dahlberg
and
the University of St. Thomas
for providing the opportunity and place
to discover the power and potential
of inventive creative thinking.

Thank you also to
Taylor Foss, Robbin Walker & Twanya Hill
for your encouragement and support.

Thanks to Reyn Guyer, inventor of
Twister™ and Nerf™, for introducing us
to the world of toys and games and also to
Glenn Karwoski of Karwoski & Courage, Minneapolis,
for encouraging us to do this work.

Mille Grazie to Dale Beane and his great Allegra Print & Imaging staff.

FINALLY

Kudissimos to Jon & Jen of *avenue B design* in Seattle
for the look and style of these pages.

FANNING ᵗʰᵉ CREATIVE SPIRIT

0 About Us

1 About You

2 What Is Creativity Anyway?

3 Stretch-ercises

4 The Practice of Inventivity

8 Things To Do
or See

9 Seven Practices
of Inventivity

7 Tools & Techniques

INVENTIVITY!

6 Key Qualities of
Creative People

5 Little Things

About Us

An Uncommon Adventure

About Us

If you look up **creativity** in the dictionary, don't be surprised if it says **"see Girsch, Charlie and Maria."** We are a husband-and-wife team who have been partners in an intriguing odyssey for more than three decades. Charlie was a Catholic priest, Maria was a nun; his training was in theology, hers was in French. For the past 25+ years, in addition to inventing six children, we have been successful, award-winning toy inventors!

On the other hand, if you look up **Inventivity,** you won't find it at all — at least, not yet — because it's a word that we have concocted to describe our own brand of **inventive creativity.** This book is about **Inventivity.**

In more than just "he-she/Mars-Venus" ways, we can be as different as night and day: Charlie needs glasses to read; Maria takes hers off. He's Pepsi, she's Coke. He's a night owl, she's an early bird. He's dark meat, she's white. We often cancel out each other's vote. But we **do** have one thing in common: we are both highly inventive and we value our creativity. We know there's no one way to be creative, and so, in this book, we have identified the things that WE do, and we've described the tools and techniques that WE use to stay inventive and creative.

About Us

Over the years, we never thought much about our creativity. Then one day came a head-slapping AHA! The fact that we had survived for so many years as *independent* inventors in the trendy, volatile, bottom-line-oriented world of toy business could only mean one thing: we must know something about creativity!

While toy inventing can be very rewarding both financially and emotionally, the down side can be equally extreme. It involves delayed gratification, constant ambiguity, lots of risk-taking and a complete dedication to a Dream-Dare-Do mentality. Toy inventing isn't just wearing clown noses and tossing Koosh™ balls around. It's hard work. Discounting the age-old classics like Monopoly™ and Nerf™, the average

About Us

new toy introduced each year will have a retail life of less than 18 months! On the other hand, the highs can be exhilarating, and the thrill of seeing our item in stores is much like giving birth to a precious child.

In our many years as product generators, we have licensed more than 200 concepts worldwide. We hold U.S. and international patents — and we have even won Germany's *Children's Game of the Year Award*.

Toy inventing is an uncommon profession. Few people know a real live toy inventor. We are a small fraternity of creatives that the industry depends heavily upon for the big ideas. In many ways we independent professionals are lucky because we aren't restricted by corporate cultures or mission statements. For us the sky's the limit, but we **do** have to keep stretching in order to reach it.

In addition to owning our toy business, we are also creativity trainers and speakers. We call ourselves "working creatives" because we continue to invent while we train and speak. If we want to keep coming up with marketably unique toy ideas, we know that we need to **"practice what we preach"** and **"preach what we practice"** on a daily basis!

About Us

We are fortunate to be able to enjoy the best of all possible worlds. We work in a creative business and we work together in our home-office studio. We hope we will be successful in sharing not only our techniques but our enthusiasm as well.

Learning to think like two toy inventors can be fun.
We promise.

Find us on the Internet

creativitycentral.com

About You

User's Guide
- Creativity test
- Being intentional
- Try it

Are You Creative?

Several years ago, we became interested in CREATIVITY both as an academic domain and as an everyday process. We agree with the experts who say that creativity is innate to all human beings. But just in case you're not convinced, we have developed a one-question creativity test. We call it the **Br**eyers **M**iggs quiz and, if you wish, you can take it right now. Are you ready?

Question:
Were you ever a child?

Scoring:
- If you answered YES, congratulations!
- You are a C, that is, Creative.

The point of this "test" is to help you remember that of course you were creative in your childhood! This creativity of yours can never leave you, though it *can* slip into hibernation. We have figured out what *we* do to be and stay creative and we are confident that these techniques can help you reclaim your own creative spirit.

How-to books are everywhere. So what will it take to know if this one is making a difference in your life? There are two ways to tell. First of all, if you use these techniques, you will find yourself with insights specific to *your* life and *your* problems. These awarenesses will make you feel freer and lighter. Secondly, you will notice yourself thinking and doing little things differently. Mark your calendar for one year from today. When that date arrives, look back and see if your approach to situations in your life is less frenzied and more focused. If you are doing even one thing differently in a year from the way you are doing it today, then ***Inventivity*** will be working for you. But always remember:

> **Inventivity is an inside job**

You can't change the world — or even your boss or your spouse. But you can change *you,* and even the littlest changes go a long way in unleashing your creativity.

About the Path to Creativity

Paths often lead across fields or into forests toward unexpected and uncharted territory. Unlike roads and highways, they are not mapped. They merely offer a sense of direction with the promise that someone has gone before. Surely this path must lead some-where. …

Somewhere is a destination unknown! Paths get us started and are usually easy to follow. But there aren't any up-front guarantees of where the path will take us. Yet, as kids (and this is worth remem-bering) we took these paths (a.k.a. shortcuts) with reckless abandon and simple enjoyment. There were even times when we were daring enough to venture off the path. Now, as adults, we have been known to fear risking a new or uncharted path. In fact, we tend to go the same way a good deal of the time. We call that kind of traveling a habit, even though it may be a good habit. However, this dedication to routine keeps us from enjoying the excitement of journeying through uncharted areas to unknown destinations.

Experienced Guides

These pages will be your map, and we will be the guides for those willing to venture off the road well traveled to discover new and exciting possibilities. Even though you are being asked to risk trying some new approaches, remember that we have gone before you and have enjoyed a playful and imaginative journey that has more than paid for the risks we have taken for all these years. While these pages will be good for bolstering your Bottom Line, you will be surprised to see their impact on your TOP LINE as your mind opens and expands to new possibilities.

T r i e d   a n d   T r u e

We have used everything in
these pages. We know it works!!

Remembered Creativity

Do you remember how, as a child, you could turn a trunk full of
old clothes into a great production, a clean wall into an easel,
and your backyard into a wonderland? If so, your journey on the
path to creativity will be a snap. There's nothing new to learn
here. If you believe you were creative as a child, then all you have
to do is REMEMBER!

Those same great powers that we accessed so recklessly in our
distant past are just resting and waiting for an opportunity to
pop out again. The creative spirit that we once enjoyed is still
available for resolving everyday issues and opportunities — big
or small, at work or at home.

Intentional Creativity

Even though we are all born creative, we have discovered that creative thinking can be *intentional*. Our success in the toy business isn't just about being lucky. We have consciously pushed our potential by using a variety of **tools that spur Inventivity.** We have filled these pages with many simple techniques that have raised the level of our thinking.

Luck favors a prepared mind.
— *Louis Pasteur*

"Try It, You'll Like It"

There's wisdom in the old cereal commercial starring **Mikey.** So follow along. Try not to get sidetracked by judgments about your own creative potential. Be courageous. Make the effort to join in for a delightful exploration of the many possibilities available to spark a refreshing flow of those good *old* creative juices. With any kind of luck you'll soon get back into the swing of imaginative, original thinking.

Please note: From time to time, we have included some blank pages for you to use. That means it's your turn to take a break, sip a cup of tea or hot chocolate, and jot down your own thoughts and ideas.

Take What You Like
& Leave the Rest

This slogan suggests that there might be things in these pages that you will _not_ find helpful. That's okay. Focus on the ones that work for you and find out from others what's working for them. Each of us is unique, and what works for Maria and/or Charlie might not work for you.

> Any path is only a path, and there is no affront, to oneself or to others, in dropping it if that is what your heart tells.
> — *Carlos Castaneda*

Good luck with your journey.

Charlie & Maria

What is creativity anyway?

- A creativity profile
- Some experts on the subject
- Make your own definition

What is creativity anyway?

There is no better place to start your exploration than to take a look at your understanding of **creativity.**

Some people don't think of themselves as creative, and that thought alone is a limiting belief which can block their ability to think or act creatively.

Every thought is creative.
— *Donald Neale Walsch*

Others believe that creativity is reserved for those involved in the visual or performing arts. Those people will often decide that their lack of an artful competence renders them uncreative. Still others will remember a time (often long ago and buried under layers of growing up) when as children they were amazingly

imaginative

&

curious

&

playful

and so they will limit creativity to child's play. But alas, these childhood interests and abilities were squirrelled away in order to accomplish the task of being hard-working, successful adults.

But there is good news! The experts agree that ***everyone is creative!*** The question is not **whether** you are creative. It's **how** you are creative.

C.A.R.E.

There is an instrument called the C.A.R.E. Profile®, developed by our friend Al Fahden for the Carlson Companies. By answering only 18 focused questions, you can determine whether you're mostly a **C**reator (thrives on generating ideas), an **A**dvancer (moves ideas through the system), a **R**efiner (insures that ideas are workable) or an **E**xecutor (makes ideas happen).

No one "type" of creative person in the C.A.R.E. Profile is better than any other and some of us are a blend of types, but real teamwork and collaboration occur when the creative strength of each person is acknowledged and utilized. That's how good ideas get better, and how better ideas get done!

❷

Right now, the important thing for you is to accept the simple fact that you are creative. Once done, you may want to review other people's definitions of creativity to see how both the famous and the not-so-famous view this phenomenal resource.

Some experts on the subject

As you read the following, note the diversity of understandings.
Then start to build, develop and refine your own definition.

Maria Girsch
Creativity is remembering
who you were as a child
and transferring that to
who you are as an adult.
Creativity is remembered
not learned.

**Mihaly
Csikszentmihalyi**
(Creativity, page 8)
Creativity is a process by
which a symbolic domain
in the culture is changed.

Webster
Create: to cause to come into existence.
Creativity: creative ability.

Harold Gardner
(The Creative Spirit, page 25)
Being creative means you do
something which is first of all
unusual, but it also makes
enough sense so that others
take it seriously.

Charlie Girsch
Creativity is the innate
potential to come to new
possibilities. It is the ability
to be original and uncom-
mon in thinking and doing.

Glenn Karwoski
Creativity is limitlessness —
because any defining of the
term limits our understanding of what it is or can be.

J. Ciardi
Creativity is the imaginatively
gifted recombination of
known elements into
something new.

Carol Goman
(*Creativity in Business,* page 2)
Creativity is bringing into
existence an idea that is
new to you.

UST Grad Student
Creativity is the
emergence of
imagination.

Make your own definition!

My definition of creativity:

Date

· ·

Definition

· ·

Thoughts/changes

2

After reviewing all these different possibilities and asking you to develop your own, we too have come up with a definition of our own brand of creativity which we call

INVENTIVITY:

**inventive creativity that
consistently produces benefits
for both the generator and
the user.**

Notes

Notes

Stretch-ercises™

**Getting into the habit of getting out of the habit
by cross-training your brain**

- Stretch-ercises for every day
- Stretch-ercises for 5-10 minute time spans
- Stretch-ercises for bigger chunks of time

Stretch-ercises™

> **stretch • er • cise** (strêch´er-síz) n. 1. A way to open one's mind for creative risk taking. 2. A fun thing to try. Also see *"Thinking out of the box."*

As you begin this journey into the world of **Inventivity,** there is no better way to **simmer your creative juices** than to start s t r e t c h i n g your brain — your creativity muscle!

The human mind, once stretched to a new idea, never goes back to its original dimension.
— *Oliver Wendell Holmes*

creativity

The **brain** is one of the finest computers ever designed. It's a super computer par excellence. Its capabilities,  speed, ability to sort information and the size of its hard disk are beyond our understanding. Yet, for the most part, we leave it idling as we wander through the stress of our daily routines. *Stretch-ercises* are simple exercises that take you out of the comfort of your daily habits, thereby forcing the brain to make new connections which in turn will cause neurons to flow. Once stretched, you will grow in your capacity and willingness to **think and act creatively.**

The brain is a beautiful thing. It wakes up with you in the morning and goes to sleep as soon as you go to work.

— *Robert Frost*

We've divided the *stretch-ercises* into three categories:

Stretches for anytime, anywhere

**STRETCHES FOR
5-10 MINUTE TIME SPANS**

Stretches for
BIGGER CHUNKS
of time

Stretches for anytime, anywhere

Stretch-ercises
five

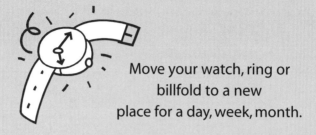

Move your watch, ring or
billfold to a new
place for a day, week, month.

3

Brainstorm 25 alternate uses for a toothpick,
toilet paper roll, newspaper, paper clip, rubber band, etc.

Make up vanity license plates or "800" numbers
for some friends and enemies.

Practice telling what you like about an idea before expressing any
concerns you might have.

Stretch-ercises
six

Listen, trying to appreciate and not judge, to a style of **music** or point of view different from what you're used to.

③

Focus on your breathing, counting from 1-10 with each exhale; start over if you lose track.

. . . .

Do all the scrabble, jumble and crossword puzzles in today's paper.

Stretch-ercises
seven

Sit in a new place for
meals, meetings,
church, temple.

3

Doodle through all your meetings and phone calls.

•

Take notes using colored pen(cil)s and maybe even on colored paper.

•

Schedule regular breaks in your day to stretch and move about.

Spend today guess-timating
measurements and distances
or who is calling when
the phone rings.

Count to 100 by **2**s and **3**s at the same time (e.g., 2/3, 4/6, 6/9, etc.) or up by **2**s and back by **3**s.

Come up with playful but appropriate responses to questions you are asked today.

Take a common object (pencil, newspaper, watch, etc.). Examine it in detail using all your senses.

Imagine and develop a conversation between a fishing lure & fish; a bee & flower; a racket & ball.

3

Take a new
or different
route
today.

3

Intentionally sleep in a
new place or position
for a few nights. Note
what happens upon
waking.

Identify all the
geometric shapes
that you can see
from where you are.

Strike up a conversation with someone you don't know or would normally avoid.

Take a walk or run, and smile at or greet each passerby.

3

Use your non-dominant hand to eat, brush your teeth, dial phone calls, etc.

Fast from the news, TV, newspaper or reading for a day.

Read the paper (or your favorite section) in a different order.

Try a new food, restaurant or recipe.

STRETCHES
FOR
5-10 MINUTE
TIME SPANS

Practice writing your name in a variety of different scripts and sizes.

•

Recall the events of yesterday and replay them across your mental TV screen.

•

Imagine yourself as someone you're not: an artist, singer, athlete, doctor, lawyer, **musician**, minority, etc.

•

Call an old friend today and reconnect.

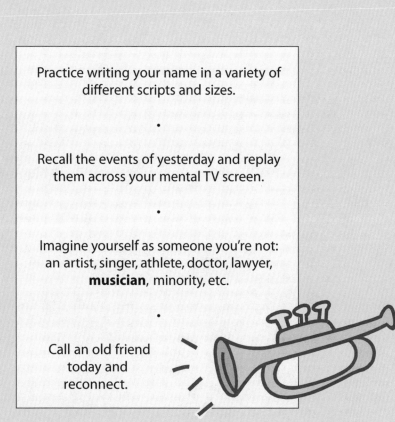

3

Take the word Thanksgiving or Christmas and see how many words you can make with the letters.

3

Imagine leading an expedition: Where are you going? With whom? With what equipment?

Use the same word in 20 consecutive sentences: *e.g.,* the word **create, risk, fear** or **courage.**

Draw an object using one continuous line without lifting pen from paper. Do it again and again.

With your eyes closed, spend a few minutes visualizing a favorite getaway place.

Take risks for a day. Risk doing *"it"* or *"something"* even when you are tempted not to.

3

Make a list in alphabetical order of descriptive words about yourself; "a" = alert, "b" = boisterous, etc.

Develop and use an affirming statement that supports the belief that you are creative.

Examine a one-frame cartoon intently for about a minute; then draw it from memory.

Draw a telephone dial or keypad from memory.

Stretch-ercises
fifteen

Make your own definition of creativity, innovation and inventing, or ask friends for theirs.

Look at an issue or opportunity from three completely different points of view.

3

Organize today by putting the important things first and be willing to let the unimportant ones go.

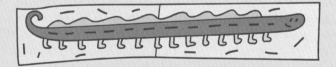

Open a dictionary randomly, pick a new word to learn and use it in your communications today.

Stretch-ercises
sixteen

Describe a combination of animals that you would like to be. Why? What would you do?

3

 **+** **+**

Spend the day giving
compliments on
clothing, work, etc.
without looking for
one in return.

Stretch-ercises
seventeen

3

With eyes closed, try to see and feel the clothes you might wear tomorrow.

Go through the alphabet naming a tool, a food and a first name for each letter.

Count the dots or freckles on your right arm, then your left.

Write up some advice for the pope, president, governor, mayor or local shop owner.

Turn on some favorite music and "direct" the music with feeling and finesse.

Draw a picture using and repeating only the number "3" or "4" or "2" etc.

Take notice of the words and body language of others in your various conversations today.

Figure out how old you are in days, weeks and months; then do dog years (x7)!

Make a list of 10-15 things for which you are grateful.

Play hooky for an hour or a day.

Check the dictionary meaning of "creativity," "courage," "curiosity," "passion," "imagination."

Do something early today that you've found yourself putting off for a while.

Make a list of 3-5 things that you could stop doing in order to simplify your life.

Make plans to take a class that interests you.

3

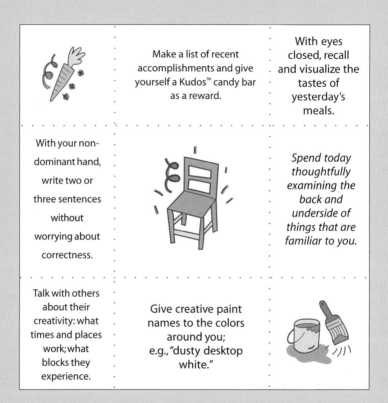

Make a list of recent accomplishments and give yourself a Kudos™ candy bar as a reward.

With eyes closed, recall and visualize the tastes of yesterday's meals.

With your non-dominant hand, write two or three sentences without worrying about correctness.

Spend today thoughtfully examining the back and underside of things that are familiar to you.

Talk with others about their creativity: what times and places work; what blocks they experience.

Give creative paint names to the colors around you; e.g., "dusty desktop white."

Put note cards/pads on your person, at your desk, in the car and at your bedside to capture ideas.

Concentrate totally on the second hand of a watch or clock without distraction for two minutes.

3

Recall and list everything you ate yesterday.

Make up subtitles for famous nursery rhymes.

Set aside at least five minutes of time in a quiet mode to do exactly nothing.

Generate 10 ideas for improving your commute, your work space, your kitchen or your next vacation.

Close your eyes for a few minutes and try to hear all the sounds going on around you.

Imagine a sound wave and watch it become music; or a TV signal and watch it become a picture.

Make a list of 20 different kinds of balls, writing utensils, seating devices, etc.

Imagine an adventure for yourself — like skydiving or running a marathon or a first date with royalty.

Recall, using all your senses, every detail of a party or celebration you've attended.

Make up a list of 20 crazy "What if?" questions.

Create fantasy solutions to a current issue or opportunity; e.g., bombing the enemy with Teddy Bears!

Mentally select the letters of the alphabet that have a horizontal, diagonal or curved element.

Spend some time with an old magazine, decorating people's faces with glasses, mustaches, etc.

Write out, and then put in order, the birth dates of your family and friends, noting which ones share dates or zodiac signs.

Record every idea you get during the course of one day.

Take apart a common appliance (like a stapler, mouse or pen) to see how it works.

Stretch-ercises
twenty-two

Examine, using all your senses, an orange, lemon, raisin,
a #2 pencil, or whatever.

Visualize in great detail your perfect work space, getaway
place, favorite car or hangout.

3

Bring to mind the face of a well-known person (Princess
Diana or Michael Jordan). Spend time watching them.

Take a 10-minute power nap or a deep-breathing relaxation
break sometime today.

Imagine for a few minutes eating a lemon or lime; or walking
on the edge of a cliff; or skydiving.

Imagine rock climbing, parasailing or bungee jumping.
What's going on in your **heart** and head?

3

Stretches for
BIGGER CHUNKS
of time

Cozy up with a cartoon
book like *The Far Side* and
chuckle away an hour.

3

Read *Tuesdays With Morrie*
and review your sense of
what is important in your life.

3

Write 20 descriptive lines about yourself using nature images: I am a leaping deer, a cotton candy cloud, etc.

Use some magazines to create a collage about yourself, about an emotion or about creativity.

Take special theme music on your next trip. When you hear it later, it will remind you of the trip.

Enjoy a long walk keenly aware of all sounds, smells, textures and variety of colors.

Take out a scrapbook or photo album. Do some remembering and reminiscing.

• • • • • • • • •

See the show *Tap Dogs* and look for the uncommon and original in the dance, music and graphics.

3

Buy a book published by *Klutz*™ about a skill you'd like to explore or learn, like juggling, watercolor, playing the harmonica — and use it!

Have a meal or take a walk with someone who inspires you.

Try on an outfit or test-drive a vehicle that is different from your present style.

Design a coat-of-arms or logo for yourself; or for a friend or loved one.

Give a good cleaning to your car or work space or any room at home!

3

See the movie *Michael* and reflect on how it offers an uncommon view of angels.

See the movie *Phenomenon* to understand the idea of being open to creativity.

See the movie *Life Is Beautiful* to witness the power of imagination in life, love and adversity.

See *Shakespeare In Love:* Imagine an English teacher using it to generate interest in Will's words and works.

See any *Harry Potter* movie for the novel storylines and the inventive language.

Wear a special scent which will bring back memories of a trip or situation that you liked.

Go to a bookstore or library and take some time to examine the art of Escher or Picasso or some other artist who intrigues you.

3

Read an article or story about three-quarters of the way through and then write your own conclusion.

Enjoy a moonlight picnic under the stars.

Invent your own Stretch-ercises:

. . . .

. . . .

. . . .

. . . .

. . . .

. . . .

. . . .

. . . .

. . . .

We'd love to hear yours.
E-mail us via our web site at **www.creativitycentral.com.**

Invent your own Stretch-ercises:

③

. . . .

. . . .

. . . .

. . . .

. . . .

. . . .

. . . .

. . . .

We'd love to hear yours.
E-mail us via our web site at **www.creativitycentral.com.**

Stretch-ercises
thirty-two

Invent your own Stretch-ercises:

. . . .

. . . .

. . . .

. . . .

. . . .

. . . .

. . . .

. . . .

. . . .

We'd love to hear yours.
E-mail us via our web site at **www.creativitycentral.com.**

The Practice
of
Inventivity

- **What if? What else? Why not?**
- **Incubation**
- **Intuition**
- **Blocks to Inventivity**

The Practice of Inventivity

In this section we will explore a handful of personal strategies we use because we believe that they support **Inventivity.**

Surely, if we claim to be creativity gurus, we must have a *"mantra"* and maybe a couple of tricks that we perform in order to deliver the biggest bang for our efforts.

What If? What Else? Why Not?

This is our mantra and definitely an easy technique to try when all else fails.

These three questions encourage you to look at any problem in a casual, almost conversational way. There is <u>no</u> challenge these questions could not speak to!

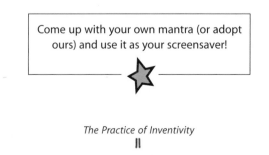

Come up with your own mantra (or adopt ours) and use it as your screensaver!

Let's start with some examples from our experience. Our Nerf™ inventing friends pulled a chunk of seat cushion foam from a ripped couch and asked WHAT IF this were a ball? WHAT ELSE could it be? Darts and cars and planes. WHY NOT? And they were off on an amazing journey shaping foam into one plaything after another.

Early in our career we found ourselves staring at one of those Fisher Price playsets and asked WHAT IF we cut it in half and put suction cups on it. WHAT ELSE? Boats, planes, school houses. WHY NOT? And we were soon collecting royalties for the Tub Town™ line.

Do you remember Ron Popeil's Pocket Fisherman? Well we found ourselves asking WHAT IF there were other pocket toys? WHAT ELSE would they be — how about a squirt gun or a kite? WHY NOT? And we had the Little Pocket Kite™.

And again, WHAT IF there were a game board through which you could probe to find a hidden squeaker? That question lead to our game called Piepmatz and ultimately to winning Germany's Children's Game of the Year Award. Just because we asked

What If?

What Else?

Why Not!!

The great thing about **What If? What Else? Why Not?** is that you already use this technique without realizing it. When you're getting dressed in the morning, for example, you may not say the exact words, but you probably get close. "**What if** I wore this green shirt with those khakis? **What else** would the shirt go with? How about these cords? Hmmm. **Why not?** Looks pretty good, actually. I'm surprised I never thought of this combination before!"

Now think about putting a meal together —
and especially when you're *missing* some ingredients. Does this sound familiar? "**What if** we have chicken and rice tonight? Oh, darn, we're out of rice. **What else** do we have that goes with chicken? Maybe these hash browns in the freezer? I've never seen 'chicken and hash browns' on a restaurant menu, but the whole family likes both chicken and hash browns. So **why not!?**"

Since you instinctively use this process on a routine basis, it's not a question of learning it, but rather of calling to mind these magic questions when you need a creative solution in some domain other than wardrobe selection or menu planning.

4

What If? What Else? Why Not? In a Nutshell

State the problem. Then ask the questions in any order.

What If? · · · · · · ·
Write down the first
things that pop into
your mind, no matter
how outrageous.

What Else? · · · · · · ·
See if you can expand
on each, either with a
brand new idea or a
variation.

Why Not? · · · · · · · · · · · · · ·
Figure out why each would <u>not</u> work.
If there's a genuine impediment,
discard that solution — but you will
be surprised at how many do-able
ideas you come up with!

Incubation: Give it a rest

Incubation is the word used by creativity gurus to describe the process of letting your thoughts and ideas simmer until that "AHA" you've been searching for is ready to pop out.

Let's face it. Most real problems are on your mind for a long time. You don't just wake up one morning and notice that your boss is a jerk or that your house is too small or that your company needs to refresh its line of widgets. They're concerns that you've been thinking about over time, and maybe for too long!

That's when you literally need to "give it a rest." Sleep on it. Or even try to forget it, which can work to your benefit — because your conscious self will get out of the way of your unconscious self, which probably had the answer all along. Go for a walk, relax in a bookstore, drive around a lake, or sit and watch a crackling fire. Those kinds of diversions are good ways to let your creative muse do the work for you.

4 Famous creative people talk about a certain time of day or a favorite place where they seem to come up with the best solutions to problems they've been pondering:

Duke Ellington wrote his best music on trains.

Descartes preferred his bed.

Hemingway haunted cafes early in the morning.

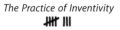

You probably know what you like to do and where you feel most peaceful, but honoring those instincts can be hard to fit into a busy day. Julia Cameron, author of *The Artist's Way,* talks about two methods of stimulating your creativity: first, to keep a **daily journal,** which she calls "Morning Pages"; and secondly, to take an "Artist's Date" once a week, that is, to do something — **totally by yourself** — that you love (or think you might love) to do. In one of her recent appearances before a big audience of her loyal fans, she asked how many were consistently keeping up with both. Quite a large number were faithful to their Morning Pages, but very few did much about their Artists' Dates!

❹

If you can spend a perfectly useless afternoon in a perfectly useless manner, you have learned how to live.
— *Lin Yutang*

Here is a fun incubation activity that we call **Magic Moments.** You need a piece of paper and three dice. (Actually, one die would do — you can probably steal one from your old Monopoly™ or Clue™ game.)

Divide the paper into three columns across and write the numbers 1-6 on the left side of the page going downwards. The first column is called "TO GO," and you should write down six different places where you like to go and can conceivably do so on a daily basis. (E.g., the bathtub is an easy daily destination; the south of France probably is not.) Next, label the middle column "TO EAT/DRINK" and write down six things you like to eat and/or drink which are easily available. Finally, call the last column "TO DO," and write down six things you enjoy doing and are possible without too much hassle (e.g., reading a novel vs. climbing a mountain).

Most likely it was easy coming up with things you like. The hard part is *doing* them. And so the Magic Moments dice will take the decision-making out of your hands and help you find some enjoyable incubation possibilities. Roll the dice (all three if you have three; otherwise, one die three times), and let one die correspond to whatever you wrote for that number in the first column, the second die refer to whatever you wrote for that number in the middle column, and the third die for the last column. Voila! You'll come up with Magic Moments like: "soak in bathtub/glass of wine/just do nothing "or" go to the park/pretzels and cheese/ride your bike "or" stay in bed/orange spice tea/listen to music." Keep rolling until you find some you really like — and then go for it!

These Magic Moments can become times and places of incubation and inspiration — and all because those little dice made you do it!

Intuition

"I wish I had listened to my intuition!"
Everyone has experienced that feeling when decisions made
against your "gut feeling" turned out to be disasters!

④

***Intuition** is knowing something without understanding why you know it.* Intuition,
like its soul mate Creativity, is a natural resource. It's a part of your makeup, and,
just like any muscle, it can be exercised and strengthened. The more you practice
your intuition, the more alert you'll be to its signals.

Your intuitive self is your faithful friend not only in personal
situations but in business as well. Professor Weston Agor's
research on intuition involved extensive interviews with
senior executives, and they overwhelmingly pointed to their
failure to listen to their own intuition as the main cause of
their worst decisions!

In addition to being your loyal friend, intuition is also your *quiet* friend. Once information is fed into your left brain, ideas and answers are everywhere, but they do need a certain amount of calm and tranquility to emerge from your right brain — which is where intuition lives. When you slow down, you're more likely to be in tune with your intuitive self.

In these moments of quiet, your direction may come in a number of ways. It could be pictures flashing in your mind, or words that you seem to hear. Many people get a physical feeling in different parts of their body, most often in their stomachs, which is probably the basis for the term "gut instinct." While you shouldn't discount the value of analytical thinking, don't forget about your built-in source of wisdom and insight.

Practicing your intuition can be as simple as remembering to ask yourself what it's telling you. But there are also some fun exercises that you can try.

4

The easiest one is simply to guess at things. When the phone rings, guess who it is before you answer. Guess who's going to win (not whom you want to win) the game tonight. Guess what your spouse is going to say about work today. Guess what the reaction will be when you deliver your weekly report.

Another exercise takes a bit more effort, but can be quite enlightening. It's called the

P¡ck-3
Process

and here's how it works.

1. First, think about your challenge, question or situation without distraction — for a few minutes.
2. Now think about your intuition for a few more minutes, and imagine it coursing throughout your whole body — in your head, your shoulders, your chest, your stomach, etc.
3. Now quickly pick any three words from the following list:

• paper clip	• sandal	• sailboat
• razor	• peach	• rubber ball
• bookmark	• tennis racket	• can opener
• candle	• camera	• shoelace
• duffle bag	• river	• car key

The Practice of Inventivity
‖‖‖ ‖‖‖ ‖‖‖

One at a time, think how each item you chose can relate symbolically to your problem. What does the candle tell you about the difficulties you're having with your partner? What meaning might the sailboat or paper clip have on whether or not you should look for a new apartment? The objects don't give answers, but they can give you insights that help you come up with the answers. Intuition is in you; the objects just access your unconscious knowledge.

You listen to other experts all the time:
authors, talk show guests,
professional authorities.
Why not listen to *your* inner voice?
It knows plenty!

Dig up all the information you can, then go with your instincts. I use my intellect to inform my instinct, then I use my instinct to test all this data. "Hey, instinct, does this sound right? Does it smell right, feel right, fit right?"
— *General Colin Powell*

Spend time every day listening to what your muse is trying to tell you.
— *St. Bartholomew*

The Last Word(s) on Intuition

The quieter you become, the more you can hear.
— *Baba Ram Dass*

4

Notice what happens when you follow your intuitive feelings. The result is usually increased energy and power, and a sense of things flowing.
— *Shakti Gawain*

We need to make the world safe for creativity and intuition, for it's creativity and intuition that will make the world safe for us.
— *Edgar Mitchell (Apollo Astronaut)*

Notes & Reflections

. . . .

. . . .

. . . .

. . . .

. . . .

. . . .

. . . .

. . . .

. . . .

. . . .

. . . .

. . . .

. . . .

Blocks to Inventivity

If everyone wants to be creative, what stops us? Bee Bleedthorn suggests the culprits are **Habit** and **Fear.** Other experts blame **Judgment, Assumptions** and **Expectations.** Still others, mind-boggled by the statistics that show a shocking creativity decrease from 98% creative at age 5 to less than 10% creative by age 30, point their fingers at **Educational, Social,** and **Cultural** factors. We often use the terms **Hurry** and **Worry** in our seminars.

❹

Whatever the vocabulary, some commonalities emerge. As the "Erroneous Zones" cartoon suggests, the blocks to creativity really *are* all in the mind! The same mind that can be a source of your great ideas can also serve as a major block to your creative efforts.

The Erroneous Zone

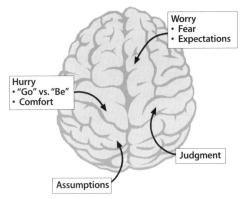

Worry
• Fear
• Expectations

Hurry
• "Go" vs. "Be"
• Comfort

Judgment

Assumptions

HURRY & HABIT

It's not difficult to experience what Michael Cole calls "busy mind" in today's fast-paced world and, as Stephen Covey points out, to get confused about what's really important. The result is **hurry.** Life in the 21st century is fast and full. Because of that reality, the human instinct for survival seeks comfort in conformity and habits. Doing things the same old way appears at first blush to offer simplicity to the complexity of life and career. But "same-old-same-old" can also rob you of the opportunities to establish the quiet times you need so that your subconscious can be jumpstarted to organize and address the challenges you face.

It's unlikely you'll ever have a hurry-free life, but half of the hustle-bustle battle is simple awareness. It's not that you *can't* slow down. You just *forget*. Here's something to try. Move your watch (or some other very familiar object if you don't wear a watch) to your other hand. Every time you look for it, remind yourself to

s-l-o-w d-o-w-n

4

In addition to becoming a frequent reminder, the very act of changing your watch is a way of stretching yourself. You're leaving your comfort zone and daring your brain to process information differently. It's such a small thing to do, but it packs a wallop to your gray matter, and nothing enjoys a challenge more than your brain.

W O R R Y & F E A R

It's not uncommon to become stymied by fear and anxiety, and as a result, you **worry.**

Fear colludes with our most conservative self and allows us to stop before we try, dismiss before we think, mock before we imagine.
— *Carol Lloyd*

Carol Lloyd says it all. Fear can paralyze your creative efforts or those of your fellow brainstormers. Fear happens when you're faced with a challenge that requires you to move from comfort to discomfort. It's easy to worry about how you will look, about how much effort will be expected, about how you will perform or about just-plain-failing. Most worry is fear-based, and it can stop you from arriving at the novel idea or the creative solution that you've been searching for.

The movie *Defending Your Life* presents an interesting look at a life lived in fear. It's enjoyable and instructive to watch Albert Brooks try to defend the fear-based choices he made to preserve and protect his life and career.

On the other hand, before you throw all caution to the wind, please note that *fear itself is not bad*. In fact, it can serve as an indication that you are about to stretch and move into the unknown — which is a mecca for stirring the creative juices. It's not fear alone that you should be concerned about, but rather how you respond in a moment of fear. The creative person simply acknowledges and accepts his or her apprehensions, and proceeds courageously into new and uncharted territory.

Minds, like bodies, will often fall into a pimpled, ill-conditioned state from mere excess of comfort.

— Charles Dickens

4

The reality is that most creative moments occur when we step out of our

CoMfort ZonE

Picasso even suggests that there needs to be destruction before there can be construction. It is helpful to understand where your individual tolerance for discomfort lies. A good way to test your own level is to note how long you were able to stand the uneasiness you felt when your watch was on your other hand. That length of time is an indication of how much discomfort you can take!

J U D G M E N T

Another very common block to creativity that we address in our seminars is judgment — that quickness to evaluate even the simplest suggestion. Again, it's a very human instinct to judge rather than support. Somehow it seems easier to kill an idea rather than support it because maybe then you won't have to get involved. What a long way we've come from our childhood willingness to try anything — even our most whimsical and unconventional ideas, or those of our playmates! Positive energy comes from using the **IQ** technique (chapter 5), which involves looking first at what **I**nterests you about an idea, and only then at the **Q**uestions or concerns you might have about it.

KILLER COMMENTS

4

Creativity is so delicate to a flower that praise tends to make it bloom while discouragement often nips it in the bud.
— Alex Osborn

There are lots of simple one-line put-downs that can quickly kill an idea. Check out the following list compiled by Min Basadur. Add others you've heard from colleagues — as well as family and friends. (Shooting down ideas is a national sport, not just a corporate custom.) But most importantly, can you hear yourself saying any of these? If so, try to be attentive to your own "killer tendencies."

Some Killer Phrases

A good idea, but ...

Costs too much.

It needs more study.

It's not part of your job.

Let's sit on it for a while.

The boss won't go for it.

The old-timers won't go for it.

We have been doing it this way for a long time.

Why hasn't someone suggested it before if it's a good idea?

Let's form a committee.

We've never done it that way.

It's been done before. (*P.S. Beanie Babies were done before. Duh!*)

ENCOURAGING WORDS

These are the opposite of killer comments. Some may be very familiar to you already, hopefully because you use them. See if you can add others to this list, and work hard to use them to nurture ideas.

Encouraging Words

Now there's a good idea.

We could do that.

Yes! And ...

Oh, I like that!

That could work.

We could try that.

There you go!

Way to go!

Now there's some good thinking!

There's a novel direction.

Cool!

The Practice of Inventivity
𝦆𝦆𝦆 𝦆𝦆𝦆 𝦆𝦆𝦆 𝦆𝦆𝦆 𝦆𝦆𝦆 IIII

EDUCATION, SOCIETY & CULTURE

These are the domains that you have the least control over, but nonetheless, it's important to realize their impact on the creative process.

During your years of **education,** didn't you often get the impression that there was only one right way to answer textbook and life questions? This is in direct opposition to the concept of generating lots of possible answers to get to the very best solution. You weren't in school long before you experienced the **social pressure** of your classmates dictating what you should wear. You may still feel judged by your  wardrobe. If it's not Polo™ or the latest name brand, you might be concerned about being ostracized and therefore spend your energy trying to conform to others' standards rather than to your own.

Finally, in your job, you often face a **corporate culture** that needs lots of rules and regulations to keep things moving ahead in an orderly fashion. Once again, you most likely find yourself giving into yet another set of pressures at the expense of your creative instincts.

4

Blocks to creativity are everywhere, and they're hard little

buggers

to overcome. But your awareness alone will go a long way in paving your personal path to creativity.

Little Things

- A.C.T. as if you are creative
- Impossible inventions
- Make more mistakes
- No more "Yes, But ..."
- Use your I.Q.
- Idea-generating guidelines
- Add color to your thinking
- Idea trapping
- The creative environment
- The A.C.E. of (Creative) Hearts

Little Things

The little things (you can do) mean a lot

Inventive creativity takes an effort, so you will need to make a decision to go the extra mile in order to get into the habit.

Here are some simple things that we have built into our days in order to assist and stimulate our creative efforts and our output. Try to be aware of the many opportunities your typical day contains to practice any or all of these.

Act as if you are creative

To ACT creative you will need:

ATTITUDE: If you answered "yes" to our Breyers Miggs quiz, you are creative. Believe it. You enjoyed your creativity as a child and you can reclaim it at anytime. Just start telling everyone that you are "creative," and then act like it. We wear our "What If?" hats everywhere and Charlie's license plate reads CRE8IVE.

COMMITMENT: You've seen the Stretch~ercises™. We are constantly trying to do the old in new ways and challenging ourselves to take different kinds of risks. We are dedicated to this practice and promise that you will be deeply rewarded if you make the same commitment.

TOOLS: In the pages that follow you will be provided with a wide assortment of tools that you can use alone or in collaboration with others to generate awesome ideas. Try them out. Practice using them and be willing to pull them out anytime that you or someone you know is stuck for ideas. This stuff really works!!

ACT as if you are creative (you are!). You will be surprised how differently people treat you.

It can be life-changing!
Really!

Impossible inventions

"There's no use trying," said Alice. "One can't believe impossible things."

"I daresay you haven't had much practice, "said the Queen. "When I was your age, I always did it for half an hour a day. Why, sometimes I've believed as many as six impossible things before breakfast."

— *Lewis Carroll*
(From *Alice in Wonderland*)

In the mindset of **Dream, Dare, Do,** one quickly realizes that it's difficult to dare or do if you haven't done some dreaming. So why not heed the queen's reminder and build some impossible ideas or inventions into your day?

Charlie tries to invent one impossible thing every day. He feels that this practice keeps him in his stretching mode, and ready to invent non-impossible things at the drop of a hat.

Today Charlie came up with a remote control mini vac to rid sinuses of pollen during the hay fever season. Last Friday he planned an airplane landing scheme using a 2,000-foot-high spiral exit ramp as a model for reducing noise.

Try it. You don't have to reveal your impossible inventions to anyone. Be careful to avoid evaluating them and we guarantee that you'll be ready, willing and able when a real-life moment calls for some daring solutions.

Keep track of your impossible ideas here:

. . . .
. . . .
. . . .
. . . .
. . . .
. . . .
. . . .
. . . .
. . . .
. . . .
. . . .
. . . .
. . . .
. . . .
. . . .
. . . .
. . . .

5

The impossible *talked of* is less impossible from the moment words are laid to it.

— *Storm Jameson*

... to dream the impossible dream ...

— *The Man of La Mancha*

I've dreamt in my life dreams that have stayed with me ever after, and changed my ideas: They've gone through and through me, like wine through water, and altered the color of my mind.

— *Emily Brontë*

5

I dream, therefore I become.

— *Cheryl Grossman*

Make more mistakes

For some unknown reason, part of the American Dream is to appear to live flawlessly, never making a mistake. While the concept has some appeal, it tends to fly in the face of one of the basic tenets of **Inventivity.** It's true that we learn plenty from  our mistakes, and so it is important to be able to make them — but we can only make mistakes if we are trying something new and different. One of our most recent mistakes happily turned into a magical toy idea for Mattel's Barbie™ line.

ooops!

If you're not failing every now and again, it's a sign you're not
doing anything very innovative.
— Woody Allen

If you made **10 mistakes a day** (even insignificant ones like dropping something) but learned some small lesson from each (like not trying to carry too many things at once), you would have learned **3,650 lessons each year.** Let mistakes be your mentors.

The history of invention is full of discoveries like *Teflon*™ or *Post-It*™ notes that were mistakenly unearthed only because the discoverer was busy in the lab working on something else.

5

No more "Yes, But ..."

Now that we've got you thinking and acting like you are creative, we need to spend a few minutes working on what NOT to say when a "new idea" comes floating through the air.

The *Ideas To Go* agency in Minneapolis gives out "No more YES, BUT!" posters, stickers and buttons. They know that this response is the quintessential way to put an idea down. How often have you felt pumped up by what seemed like a supportive YES only to hear it quickly followed by a deflating BUT!?

When you're tempted to say YES, BUT, try YES, AND instead.

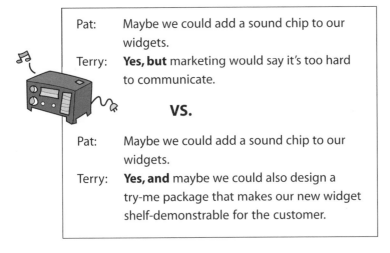

For example:

Pat: Maybe we could add a sound chip to our widgets.

Terry: **Yes, but** marketing would say it's too hard to communicate.

VS.

Pat: Maybe we could add a sound chip to our widgets.

Terry: **Yes, and** maybe we could also design a try-me package that makes our new widget shelf-demonstrable for the customer.

❺

The first example puts an immediate damper on Pat's idea. The second example keeps it alive. Very few ideas are perfect in their original iteration anyway. They need to be twisted and tweaked in order to become do-able. **Yes, and** promotes collaboration and everyone feels like a winner in the end.

Use Your I.Q.

To Talk About The Pluses First!

The truth of the matter is that when an idea is proposed these days, the odds are that the proposer will get at least **four negative** responses before getting **one positive** one. When you are reviewing a new idea, get in the habit of first talking about what **I**nterests, **I**ntrigues and **I**nspires you about it before bringing up your **Q**uestions or concerns (and the latter *only* in the form of a query!).

5

INTERESTS
QUESTIONS

It takes courage to be creative. As soon as you have a new idea, you are in a minority of one.

— *Paul Torrance*

The **I.Q.** technique is really a simple practice that's easy to execute and guaranteed to honor new ideas. Here's how it works.

Let's say the question is:

"What would happen if we had a national leave-your-car-at-home day?"

INTERESTS

Note what you like about the idea. What excites or intrigues you? What does it inspire you to accomplish? What do you see as unique? Start by saying *I find this idea interesting because.............* or *I like that.........*

- *I like that it would let people see firsthand how it would be to get along without their cars.*
- *I'm interested in the positive effect it would have on the environment.*
- *I think it would inspire me to get some exercise that I don't get in my car.*

INTRIGUE AND INSPIRATION

The intrigue and inspiration aspect encourages you to expand the idea as you think about what "could be" if this suggestion were ever to happen. Would this idea offer any benefits or advantages that nobody's thought about before? Continue the **I** of **IQ** by focusing on the **potentials** of the idea.

- *I'm intrigued by the fact that people might actually come to prefer alternate forms of transportation which they would never have previously given serious thought to.*
- *I wonder if a successful leave-your-car-at-home day would encourage other days like that throughout the year.*
- *It might actually reduce the cost of insurance and ownership.*

QUESTIONS

Your apprehensions should not be ignored. The **Q** of the **I.Q.** approach encourages you to state your concerns. However, rather than using killer comments like "We don't have the money," or "So-and-so won't like it," force yourself to put your reservations in the form of a question to be resolved, rather than a problem to be dismissed.

Use phrases like *In what way might I/we...?* or *How might I/we...?*

- *How would we get cooperation from people who just don't want to give up their car for a day?*
- *What would we do in case of an emergency?*
- *What type of vehicles would be exempt?*

5

I.Q. in a Nutshell
Review ideas in this order:

Communicate what catches your interest. $\longrightarrow$ Explore the potentials that intrigue or inspire you. $\longrightarrow$ Address concerns in the form of a question to be resolved.

There are a couple of twists on this approach:

1. Creativity guru Edward de Bono prefers the following alternative:
   - **Positives:** Talk about the upside potential.
   - **Negatives:** Account for people's concerns.
   - **Interesting:** Get a big-picture view of the possibilities.

2. Multiple Resources Associates designed a P.P.C. model based on Aristotle's pluses and minuses of an idea:
   - **P - Pluses:** what you like.
   - **P - Potentials:** what could be.
   - **C - Concerns:** what you're worried about.

   All of these methods work. Pick your favorite.

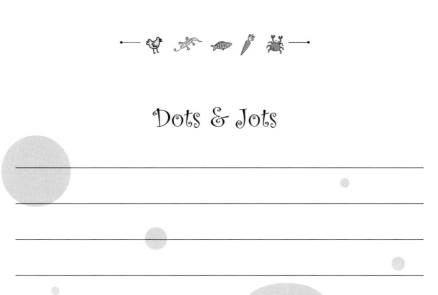

Dots & Jots

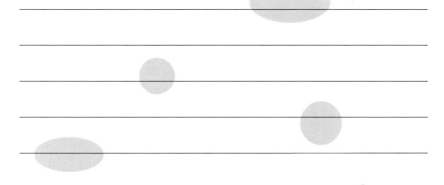

5

Idea-generating guidelines

Fishing With a Net

Age-old wisdom suggests that teaching a man *how* to fish is much better than giving him a fish. Here's *how to fish for ideas* as well as some simple advice on how to get the most out of your efforts.

For starters, think "net" versus "bobber and line." The effect is obvious as nets pull in lots of fish from which to pick and choose, while a line catches one fish at a time. That fish must then be examined by itself (and not in relation to other fish) when deciding whether it's a keeper.

Here are eight idea-generating guidelines to help you pull in a net full of ideas.

1. Generate lots and lots of possibilities

More is definitely better. A friend of ours, Dr. Paul Marsnik at the University of St. John, has spent quite a few years recording and evaluating the output of two different control groups.

The first group was charged with getting *lots* of ideas, the second with getting the *best* possible idea. Without fail, the independent judges found that the better-quality ideas came from the group that produced the most ideas. More *is* better.

The sister cities of Zurich and Chicago have demonstrated this principle with their similar COWS exhibits. Chicago gave 300 full-sized plastic cows to 300 artists to paint, decorate or embellish in any way they chose. Needless to say, not one duplicate arose. For us, it's proof-positive that there are lots of ways to do anything.

2. Defer judgment at all costs

The St. John's study also observed that those trying to get the "best idea" got bogged down in judging their output — so much so that they were stifled, and therefore limited, in the number of ideas they were even able to generate. So, do what you can to avoid judging your own or others' ideas. And watch out for those killer phrases like "done before" or "costs too much" or "it'll never get by so and so." Just keep the flow of ideas going until you have at least 20 or 30 or more.

> The only difference between a weed and a flower is judgment.
> — *Unknown*

3. Be wild and crazy

Have fun. Life is difficult enough, and a little craziness (if not judged) often gives permission for more "out of the box" thinking. Since judging is taboo, don't be afraid to be outrageous!

4. Piggyback on other people's ideas

In school, copying was cheating, but in the idea-generating business one good idea often *leads* you or someone else to other good ideas when you build upon what has been said before.

5

5. Have a positive, constructive attitude

Gently affirming another's suggestion with "YES, and we could ..." or "We could do that" or "That could work" opens the door to a greater flow than those energy-sapping "killer" comments mentioned earlier. It also encourages others to take the risk of adding (rather than editing) anything that comes to mind. Just try to make simple declarative statements to keep everything moving ahead.

6. Avoid breaking the flow

Long, drawn-out explanations or unimportant technical inquiries can cramp a brainstorming session. Keep in mind that starting your idea with a question like "Could we ... " or " What if we ..." becomes an invitation for someone to break the flow in order to answer your inquiry. When you're in this initial generating stage, it's better to just blurt out ideas as they come.

⑤

7. Promise convergence

There are some people who find fishing for lots of ideas difficult. It is helpful to assure them that there *will* be a time to evaluate the output, apply the necessary criteria, and select the very best possibilities.

8. Keep it light

It's not a perfect world, and there will be times when interruptions with questions, judgments or commentary break the flow. At those times it's often helpful to diffuse these with a little playful counterattack. We suggest using Koosh™ or Nerf™ balls, paper wads, stickers or humor to toss at the flow-breakers.

Brain waves

Adding

to your Inventivity

5

Inventive creativity, which is about *spirit* and *energy*, struggles in a black-and-white, linear world. In fact, it's many of the left-brained rules and regulations you are exposed to that wreak havoc with your **creative instincts.**

Add to that the typical workplace stress of downsizing, endless meetings, performance reviews and bottom lines, and it's a wonder that your right-brained activities ever see the light of day!

Here's a very simple way to make waves in the right side of your brain:

Recall how the sight of fall colors or a beautiful **rainbow** can take your breath away. That's because they're speaking to your visual, artistic and playful right brain. Why not keep it stimulated by adding some **COLOR** to your day with colored pens (BIC™ and Pilot™ sell inexpensive four-color pens), paper, clips and other stationery items. Speaking of color, check out our **Think Pen** technique in chapter 7.

We all went off to kindergarten with a magical box of color crayons and graduated from high school with a disposable ball point pen.

Idea trapping

The brain and our subconscious are **Inventivity** helpers.
Properly stimulated, these two can assist in idea generation and
problem solving.

Honoring Ideas

Mike Veeck tells a story about his father, Bill Veeck, the baseball legend
known for making the game more entertaining for the fans. His dad
kept all of his ideas for improving the game on little index cards in a file
box in the family study. There were nine children. (Mike says there
might have been 10 if the designated
hitter rule had been in force in those
days!) They lived in an old frame
home. Because the house was a
bit of a firetrap, they had an escape
plan so that everyone could get out in
case of a fire.

Each of the older children was responsible for one of the younger ones, and the oldest sister had the singular responsibility of safely rescuing the file box full of ideas to revolutionize baseball. They honored those ideas!

Tapping the Subconscious

One of the most exciting possibilities of **Inventivity** is to learn to use and trust the power of the subconscious. You have a friend in your mind's ability to organize all the information recorded in your memories. Learning to arrange your creative-thinking efforts to be able to utilize this potential is most desirable. Both incubation and idea trapping are easy ways to access and hold onto your EUREKAs and AHAs!

> Inspiration is everywhere if you're willing to recognize it and let it move you.
> — *James Bell*

Incubation

Incubation, as previously noted, is nothing more than **sleeping on your dreams and schemes.** Keep in mind the proclivity of the subconscious to organize all the stuff that is floating around in your mind. The invitation here is to let your subconscious sort through and make use of its multitude of unrelated pieces of stored information in your search for uncommon solutions.

5

Idea Trapping in a Nutshell

 Identify the challenge.

 Write down the facts you already know or need to know about the challenge.

 Now rewrite the challenge in question form a number of times and choose the best one. Try starting with:
- *How might we ...*
- *In what ways might we ...*

5

 Sleep on it. Put your question in your purse or pocket, but stop thinking about it and see what comes.

 You'll be surprised at how many ideas come to you. Be sure to write them down, noting where you are and what time of day they occurred.

Conduct your own test.
You can copy the following form. Fill it in, carry it with you, and use it for as long as you need or like.

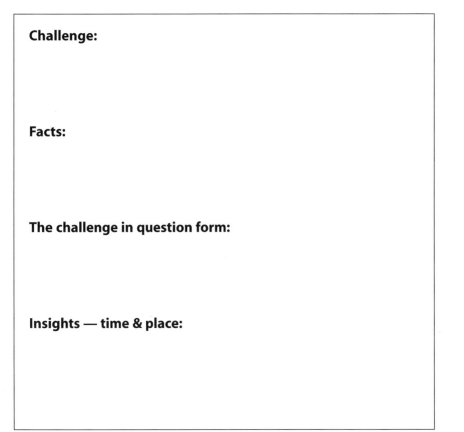

Idea trapping

Challenge:

Facts:

The challenge in question form:

Insights — time & place:

5

The creative environment

While there is no official Martha Stewart for the creativity movement to tell you how to decorate your space (and Maria is not yet willing to serve), our experience is that the more stimulating your environment is, the more productive you will be. Ad agencies and design firms value a creative climate, and they often go the extra mile to spiff up their surroundings.

Anything that helps to get the juices flowing, without getting in the way, works. There are many ways to excite the spirit. Color, play and music are just a few. In our studio we keep lots of **toys and novelties** around (and not just because we're toy inventors). Today you can purchase keychain replicas of the classic toys and games we all grew up with — and best of all, they really work.

Music is a dynamic way to influence your surroundings. From the soothing to the energetic, the options are unlimited. Sound can do much to create a mood or energy for a productive atmosphere. **Art and color** can also become a catalyst by visually touching the right side of your brain.

5

In addition to designing a creative climate, you may also want to keep adding to or changing it on a regular basis. Use whatever turns you on at the time. Take a hard look at your surroundings, and do what you can to establish a resourceful and friendly environment for yourself and others.

The
A.C.E.

Of (creative) Hearts.

"There's nothing new under the sun."

Whoever said that believes that everything which appears to be new is really a combination of existing parts and pieces. He or she may be right.

We too have noticed both in and out of the toy industry that the simplest gee-whiz products or services are often **a**daptions, **c**ombinations or **e**xaggerations of things that already exist. And so, we have invented an acronym called **A.C.E.**

Here's how to A.C.E. your next idea-generating sesssion:

ADAPT

To **adapt** something means to alter its form, composition, materials or manufacturing process (in the case of a product) or to modify its uses or benefits (in the case of a service). The common chair is a perfect example. Think about it. The "essence of chair" in most people's minds probably includes four legs, a back, and a seat about 18 inches from the floor. Now review how people have **adapted** the basic chair over time as you visualize beanbag chairs, inflatable chairs, stools, hammocks, wheelchairs, ergonomic desk chairs and folding chairs to name but a few. In many cases, the inventor adapted not only the materials or manufacturing process, but also the use.

One of our most successful toy inventions is a bath item called *TubTown*™. We adapted traditional tub play (rubber ducky... splash, splash...) to figure play by designing a "harbor village" that suction-cups to the side of the tub. Now Johnny or Suzie can have hours of bathtime fun with the many features that a playset offers, and Mom likes the off-to-the-side, no-mess containment that the suction cups provide.

Try it yourself. Think about something very common like a ball— and see how many adaptations you can come up with. Now try the same process with one of your own personal or professional challenges.

COMBINE

To **combine** means simply to take two existing things and join them to make something new. Examples of classic combos include the *clock radio*, the *wristwatch*, the *motorhome*, the *toaster oven* and the *umbrella stroller*. The world is full of these types of marriages and if you just look around you right now, chances are there's a notable combination nearby.

5

Another of our best-selling toy inventions is an item called the *Wrist Racer*. When Johnny and Suzie wind their chunky, oversized watch, they're really winding up the mini car beneath its crystal. When they pull out the concealed ramp and press the release button, their racer shoots out across the floor, and even does stunts! Nothing new here. We didn't invent racers and we didn't invent wrists! But the marriage of the two made *Wrist Racers* a runaway take-off!!

5

A quick way to try your own hand at combining is to pick any two things at random and imagine some sort of new product that could result if they were blended. Maybe, by chance, you'll come up with the next eureka invention. In Chapter Seven we expand the combining process in more detail with two techniques called *Click Cards* and *Toying Around*.

EXAGGERATE

5

To **exaggerate** is probably the most fun of the three, because the sky's the limit here. It's simple. Take an item and go nuts! **Exaggerate** it to its most outrageous degree, even if the results are offensive.

In Toy Biz, there's a category we call "Scary, Gross and Yukky." It includes things like monsters and aliens and slime and goop. One of our toy exaggerations is an item called *Bad Eggz* which sold extensively in Europe. Each egg contains a surprise inside. When the child cracks or squeezes it open, a collectible creature is revealed inside of the egg's goopy slime. It's scary, gross and yukky all wrapped up in one— and kids love it!

5

Again, try it yourself by looking around you. Exaggerate the look or use of a spoon. What crazy thing could a showerhead do? Now try it with a service. If the United States Post Office were to add some outrageous benefit to its customers, what might it be?

One of our all time favorite brainstorming methods essentially uses this process. We call it the **Get Your Butt Fired Technique** and you can find out more about it in Chapter 7. The reason people enjoy this approach so much is because it grants the rare permission to be outlandish—a treat adulthood seldom encourages. You not only pass "Go," but you can proceed immediately to "out of the box" thinking. Let's face it. It's just plain fun to be extreme, offensive, and even disgusting!

Because the **A.C.E.** approach is so quick and easy and fun, don't forget to use it as a Stretch-ercise. Start **A.C.E.-**ing objects around you. Keep remembering to ask yourself "How can I **adapt**, **combine** and **exaggerate** this pencil or that stop sign or the milk carton the kids left out on the counter?" As you practice and enjoy this process, it may turn you into an "ace" brainstormer!

⑤

A.C.E. In A Nutshell

- Identify the item or idea you want to change.
- First, consider altering its form, its composition, its benefit or its use.
- Next, think about combining it with something else to establish a new direction.
- Finally, exaggerate it until you come up with a novel orientation or position.

Key Qualities
of
Creative People

They are
- **Willing to generate lots of ideas**
- **Curious**
- **Aware and observant**
- **Improvisers and risk-takers**
- **Able to see the "old" in new ways**
- **Dreamers**
- **Fun-loving**
- **Able to live with ambiguity**

Key Qualities
of
Creative People

Through the years we have come to understand that creative people demonstrate certain qualities that distinguish them from those who choose **not** to think and act as if they are creative.

We will briefly explore the essence of some of these qualities, suggest an exercise or two, and note a few **Stretch-ercises**™ that will help you practice the quality.

Creative people are willing to generate lots of ideas

Innovators seldom stop with the first idea that comes to them. They persist and push themselves to come up with 15, 30 or more ideas, confident that the results will improve with the variety of al- ternatives they achieve. They understand that *"lots lead to better"* and are willing to make the effort in order to get the bright idea. They trust that the real break- throughs come when the mind begins to flex and discover new and original possibilities.

6

Here is a simple stretch-ercise. Take something common like a newspaper, tongue depressor, toilet paper roll, kitchen utensil, glass, pencil or paper clip, and ask yourself, "What else could this be?" Push yourself to go for 25 or more ideas.

Look
at things differently

Hint: When new ideas are slow to come, change your Point of View **(POV).** How would it be used in the classroom or at worship? What would a politician or a customer, a sales person or a fashion model do with it? What could you do with it in the garden or on an airplane? What if it were bigger or smaller? And so on... Just keep changing your perspective - kind of like when you looked at the world through your legs as a child. Be careful you don't tip over!!

Key Qualities of Creative People

Creative people are inquisitive & curious

Curiosity may have killed the cat, but the invention annals are full of amazing discoveries that came about in moments of curious exploration.

It is said that necessity is the mother of
invention, but there has been a curious lack of
interest in discovering the father.
Could it be that the father is curiosity?
— *Eugene Raudseep*

HOW COME?

Kids are famous for their HOW COME? questions. Remembering our childhood creativity should help us practice this quality. Just take a normal situation and ask How come? questions until you move past the obvious into a realm of amazing and entertaining possibilities.

Mr. Smith went to a school in the middle of the day, in the middle of the week, but he didn't see any children there.

HOW COME?

Now see if you can write down 15 or 20 real or imagined answers for this query.

> **HINT**
> Remember to look at the object from a
> variety of different perspectives!

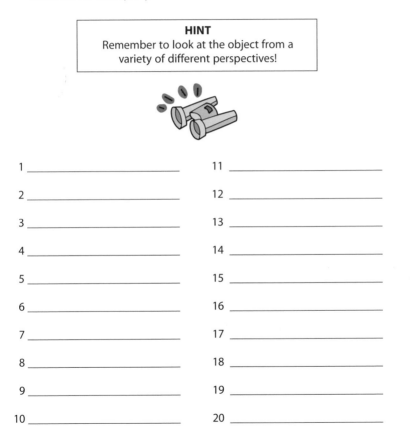

1 _____

2 _____

3 _____

4 _____

5 _____

6 _____

7 _____

8 _____

9 _____

10 _____

11 _____

12 _____

13 _____

14 _____

15 _____

16 _____

17 _____

18 _____

19 _____

20 _____

6

So, how did you do?

Did you persist until 20?

•

Were you able to get beyond the common possibilities of vacation or field trip or fire drill?

•

Were you able to get a little further out with things like alien invasions or bizarre Halloween capers?

•

Were you able to think of different kinds of schools — like night school, or school of fish?

Curiosity is one of the permanent and certain characteristics of a vigorous intellect.
—*Samuel Johnson*

*Just remember that **quantity** will lead to new perspectives. which often lead to some very original possibilities.*

Some more HOW COME? questions for you to try:

**The Shorts were supposed to leave on their vacation this morning, but they're still home.
HOW COME?**

**Mrs. Nightingale has tea every afternoon at four, but today she didn't.
HOW COME?**

**Pat was on the highway, but the traffic was barely moving.
HOW COME?**

6

The "silly question" is the first intimation of some totally new development.
— *Alfred North Whitehead*

s t r e t c h - e r c i s e s

To get those curiousity juices flowing

Write out the birthdates of your friends and relatives in chronological order, beginning with the oldest. See how many people share dates or signs.

Make up a list of 5 or 10
How Come? questions.

Figure out how old you are in minutes, hours, days, weeks and months. Then do dog years (x7)!

Take apart a common appliance, like a stapler or pen or even something a little more intricate.

Oodles of doodles

Creative people are aware & observant

Life is in the details. This is also true of **Inventivity.** So often, the day's pace and routines keep us from simple awarenesses that can broaden our appreciations and our ability to think more creatively.

An old cliche suggests that we ought to "stop and smell the roses." A perfect way to exercise this quality is to take a common object and become intimately familiar with it.

6

Can you find the symbol of the Federal Express service within their logo?

Answer: an arrow between the E and x.

Let's try it.

Using all your senses, take a long, thoughtful look at a good old #2 pencil. Pick it up and stare at it.

What colors do you see?

Rub your fingers over it. What do you feel?

What details stand out?

How does it look when you hold it in different positions?

Are there special marks that set it apart from other pencils?

Hold it up to your nose. How does it smell? at the top? at the point?

Touch it to your tongue. How does it taste and feel?

6

Does it seem that you are now best friends with your #2 pencil? Hopefully, you have gained an appreciation that you didn't have before — by taking the time to observe so fully this common, everyday object.

s t r e t c h - e r c i s e s

To develop awareness and observation skills

Recall, using all of your senses, a special party
or celebration you took part in.

•

Identify all the geometric shapes in your present surroundings.

•

Count the dots and freckles on your right and left forearms.

•

Spend a day noticing the words and body
language of others in your various conversations.

•

Take a long walk, alerting all
of your senses to the sounds,
smells, textures and shades
of color around you.

Creative people are improvisers & risk-takers

Did you ever watch Jonathan Winters or Robin Williams improvise? Or a couple of musicians jamming? These entertainers are legendary for their *willingness* (notice we didn't say ability) to go without a script or sheets of music, trusting that not only will they survive, but that they will delight themselves and their audience.

Improvise. **Birds** do it, kids and jazz musicians do it. Why, even middle-aged adults do it when they "make up" little excuses for being late. Our hope is that you might be willing to take the creative risk of improvising in order to tap into another dimension of your **Inventivity.**

6

> You have brains in your head.
> You have feet in your shoes.
> You can steer yourself
> Any direction you choose....
>
> ... And when things start to happen,
> Don't worry. Don't stew.
> Just go right along.
> You'll start happening, too.
>
> — *Dr. Seuss*

What we're addressing and encouraging here is the notion that there are people who improvise their way through life and enjoy the process. Also, we would like you to give yourself credit for improvising every time you negotiate through **traffic,** pick up a phone, or generally move away from a scripted activity. We are hoping that you can bring that same energy to other parts of your life without being stopped by the fear that you might fail.

Improvisation can be either a last resort or an established way of evoking creativity.
— *Mary Catherine Bateson*

Risk and change have no constituency.
— *Anonymous*

s t r e t c h - e r c i s e s

To develop your improvisational skills

Improvise playful suggestions
(where appropriate) in answer to all the
questions you are asked today.

•

Create fantasy solutions for a current issue:
Bomb the enemy with Teddy Bears; fill the
barrels of guns with hot glue sticks.

•

Make up a list of 15 or 20
"What if" questions, and try them out on
your friends and coworkers.

•

Take an old magazine and decorate or mark
up the faces of people in the ads.

Creative people see the "old" in new ways

The experts talk about approaching projects and situations with "beginner's eyes" or the "mind of a child. " Each of these images illustrates this quality. As toy inventors, we know the power of being able to see through or into an object until it assumes a new form or identity.

Take the concept of a **bike** or trike. It's a good thing toy inventors didn't accept the limitation of two or three wheels. Otherwise, we would never have seen the trike turned upside down to become the BIG WHEEL or a scooter-minus-steering with a few more wheels becoming a SKATEBOARD.

A Dodge commercial illustrates this kind of thinking:

Dodge TV Ad

Look what we're up to NOW!

We're covering new ground.

We're stirring things up.

We're making an impression

We thought of everything.

We're opening up possibilities.

We're questioning everything.

We're changing everything.

Again.

We're changing the rules.

We're not about to stop now.

s t r e t c h - e r c i s e s

To develop your ability to see the old in new ways

Examine, using all your senses, an orange,
a lemon or a lime to see it like you've
never seen it before.

•

Read a news story and then rewrite the
headline from a variety of political, social
and religious points of view.

•

Make a list of 20 different kinds of balls,
writing utensils, seating devices, etc.

Creative people are dreamers, able to visualize

> **Imagination is more important than knowledge.**
> — *Albert Einstein*

The power of this quote lies in its source. One of the most knowledgeable and influential minds of our time advised us that knowledge is not as important as the ability to dream and visualize. To prove his conviction, Einstein admitted to imagining himself riding on light beams as he invented his theory of relativity.

Do what you can to stretch your imagination and dream things that someday in some way you might dare to do. Develop your power of *"What if."*

s t r e t c h - e r c i s e s

To develop your imagination

Imagine a conversation between a bee and a flower or a
fishing lure and a fish.

•

Bring to mind the face of some well-known
person (Princess Diana or Michael Jordan).
Spend time watching them perform.

•

Describe in detail how you would spend the
next year if you won the lottery or became terminally ill.

•

Imagine an adventure for yourself — skydiving,
a date with royalty, competing in an important race.
What's going on in your head and your heart?

Creative people are fun-loving

There is power in fun, play and humor. Life is hard enough — and our downsized world has put huge pressures on our ability to enjoy our work and our lives. Let humor enter your day-to-day activities to generate an open, relaxed atmosphere. You'll feel loose. Therefore you'll be willing to take risks, to improvise, to be creative.

A University of Michigan study reveals that **children laugh 150 times** a day (which has the same effect as 15 minutes of riding a stationary bike) while **adults laugh 15 times** a day.

6

What makes laughing so healthy?

Endorphins!

Laughter releases free, legal, pain-killing uppers into our bodies. This "drug" stimulates circulation by increasing respiration, thereby producing a form of internal massage. Think about it! No, on second thought, laugh about it!

Laughter is the jam on the toast of life. It adds flavor, keeps it from being too dry and makes it easier to swallow.
— *Diane Johnson*

Appropriate Humor:
humor that is done
in good taste and
good spirit.

Inappropriate Humor:
mean-spirited
criticisms, insults or
name-calling.

6

s t r e t c h - e r c i s e s

To develop your sense of humor and play

Read the comics in your newspaper, clipping anything that tickles your funny bone to bring to work.

Share appropriate jokes with friends.

Pass along Internet humor if it strikes you as funny.

6

Creative people are able to live with ambiguity

We already know that it's not easy to be creative. It takes courage. Still, the creative person develops a tolerance for the challenge and a willingness to hang in there.

> When you get to the end of your rope, tie a knot and hang on. And swing!
> — Leo Buscaglia

A huge piece of **Inventivity** is the willingness to live without answers, to be suspended in ambiguity, and to not let the discomfort force you to quit before the spark of originality occurs.

Toy inventing teaches us a lot about ambiguity. We have licensed more than 200 concepts worldwide, but only 100 have made it to the retail shelves and probably only 10 have essentially paid the bills. It takes faith to live with the surprises and setbacks of life — the tension of ambiguity.

6

s t r e t c h - e r c i s e s

To develop tolerance for ambiguity

Work all the puzzles in the daily paper.

•

Count to 100 by 2s and 3s at the same time; and then backwards by 3s and 4s.

•

Try to answer riddles or solve mysteries.

•

Play the game Mind Trap™ and use the cards to challenge your thinking.

•

 Mentally select the letters of the alphabet that have a horizontal, diagonal or curved element.

Scribbles & Squiggles

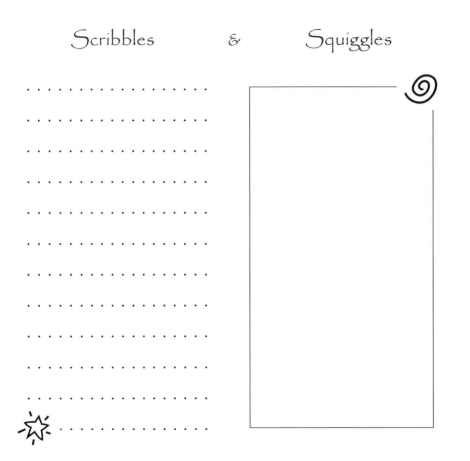

Tools & Techniques

- S.T.O.R.M.
- Think Pen
- Mind Mapping
- Forced Connections
- Click Cards
- Assumptions
- Fairy Tales
- Get Your Butt Fired!

Tools & Techniques

S.T.O.R.M.

There is a famous problem-solving model developed by Sid Parnes and Alex Osborn, two pioneers of the creativity movement. In fact, Osborn, the "O" of BBDO Advertising, is the person credited with coining the term "brainstorming." They call their method CPS (Creative Problem Solving), and it's designed as a step-by-step approach to arrive at workable solutions to any problem.

Very simply, the users first establish the **facts,** then formulate an accurate **statement of the challenge,** then originate a variety of **ideas,** then **evaluate** these ideas against agreed-upon criteria, and, finally, firm up a plan of **action.**

7

We use a similar process as an **Inventivity** tool, and have chosen the word **STORM** as its acronym. Our method also has five steps, and its power lies in the dance between *diverging* (going out) and then *converging* (coming back in) to come up with the best solution. This diverge/converge pattern occurs in each step. Pages, even books, have been written about the CPS process, but here's a quick overview of how it works.

7

STATE
the facts

Every challenge is surrounded by critical information that needs to be shared if you expect participants to deliver their best thinking. So be like Sergeant Friday of the classic TV show *Dragnet,* and go for "the facts, Ma'am, just the facts!" Write down everything you can think of that is or should be known about your issue or opportunity.

TUNE UP
the question

This very important step acknowledges that 10 people will often have 10 different ideas of what the problem or challenge is. It is extremely important to list all the possibilities, and then converge as a group on one clean and accurate statement of what you're really working on. This step makes sure everyone is on the same page.

ORIGINATE
lots of Ideas

Once the facts are in and the question is clear, start generating lots of ideas. Come up with as many as time allows, then converge down to what people choose as the top 5, 10, etc. One way to do this is to write all the ideas on flip-chart paper, tape these sheets on the wall, and give everyone five Post-It™ notes or stickers to put on their five favorite ideas. The ones that have the most "votes" are the ones you bring into the next step.

REDUCE
the possibilities

It's pedal-to-the-metal time. You have a given amount of ideas, and now you have to further reduce them. Decide on four or five factors that you will weigh each idea against. These might be things like **cost, timing, materials, capabilities,** etc. Put each idea up against all of these criteria, and usually the best one (maybe two) will emerge.

7

m

MAP OUT
a plan of action

Now you need to put your best idea into action. Figure out where the help or resistance might lie in your organization. Know where the funding might come from. Give out assignments and develop a process for reviewing the progress of your efforts. It's time to make things happen while gaining support and champions for the final idea.

7

S.T.O.R.M. is a straightforward blueprint for any **brainSTORMing**

efforts that require originality and viability. Because this is a

systematic process, the left-brained folks will feel

like you've truly covered all the bases, and the

right-brainers will be thrilled with the

creativity of the process as well

as the final resolution.

7

The Think Pen™

Edward de Bono, the author of *Six Thinking Hats,* encourages the wearing of different-colored hats when processing a challenge or opportunity as a simple reminder that there are many aspects to the creative thinking process. His suggestion is to don a hat of a specific color to keep participants focused on one aspect of the issue at a time. This becomes a manageable way for *"thinking through"* all aspects of a challenge.

We have applied the K.I.S.S. (Keep It Simple, Stupid!) principle to de Bono's technique in order to arrive at our four-color THINK PEN.™ Here's how it works:

1 Identify a challenge to be addressed

2 Take a four-color pen

3 Recall the four basic elements: Earth, Air, Water and Fire

4 Process the issue or opportunity using the following color scheme:

- BLACK (Earth) is about being *grounded in the facts.* Note all the facts concerning your challenge.

- GREEN (Air) is about *flying.* Explore the possibilities and potentials of your challenge.

- BLUE (Water) is about *blending and dissolving.* Resolve any cautions or concerns through the use of questions.

- RED (Fire) is about *energy and passion.* Identify the emotional, intuitive and sensual aspects.

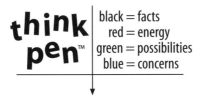

think pen™ | black = facts
red = energy
green = possibilities
blue = concerns

The Benefits:

- The four colors relate to the four universally recognized elements, making the system easy to remember.

- BIC™ and Pilot™ just happen to make an inexpensive four-color pen.

- It's a simple, productive way to visualize your thinking process, thereby providing a "big picture" look at your issue.

- BOTTOM LINE: Four colors, one pen, no hats — AND it's a fun, playful and effective tool!

Enjoy the Think Pen™ Technique...
Use it to add color to all your efforts...
Use it to identify and clarify your thinking...
Use it for the fun of it...

*One of our clients, Fortis Insurance,
has adopted our Think Pen™ method as
a corporate decision-making tool.*

Think Pen™ Example

Our friend David Hazelip is a smoking cessation counselor and likes this technique for his clients.

The Issue or Opportunity: <u>Quitting Smoking</u>

Black (Note Facts)	**Green (Explore Possibilities)**
Quitting is difficult. Cigarettes are expensive. Quitting aids are readily available. There are fewer places where smoking is allowed.	I might get rid of this cough. I won't smell like smoke. I'll save money. I won't be embarrassed or apologetic about smoking.
I would be so proud of myself if I could quit. I really, really wish I had never started. I want to feel vibrant and healthy.	What can I do to avoid failing? How might I deal with my cravings? In what ways can I manage weight gain? How can I prepare to be around smoking friends?
Red (Identify Energy)	**Blue (Question & Resolve)**

7

Think Pen™ Worksheet

The Issue or Opportunity: _____

| **Black (Note Facts)** | **Green (Explore Possibilities)** |

7

| **Red (Identify Energy)** | **Blue (Question & Resolve)** |

Think Pen™ Worksheet

The Issue or Opportunity: _____

Black (Note Facts)

Green (Explore Possibilities)

Red (Identify Energy)

Blue (Question & Resolve)

7

Mind Mapping

Mind Mapping (sometimes called Webbing) is a natural, brain-friendly way to organize your **inventive creativity.** Once you begin to appreciate the mind's ability to give order to your thoughts, you open yourself to the possibility of a more holistic approach to processing information.

The invitation here is to drain the brain quickly and painlessly of all that it knows in order to diagram your thoughts on paper. You essentially capture the flow of information, possibilities, energies, instincts and concerns through the use of:

| **1** | simple key words, phrases or symbols |

| **2** | color (if possible) |

| **3** | interconnected lines |

Think of mapping
as doodling
with a purpose

Both sides of your brain can freely associate with a topic in a simple and natural manner.

Recall a spider's web or the root system of a leafy tree, and you will begin to see what a map or web might look like. While color is not necessary, you might find it helpful.

This is Charlie's favorite technique and here is his
Mind Map on — why not? — Mind Mapping!

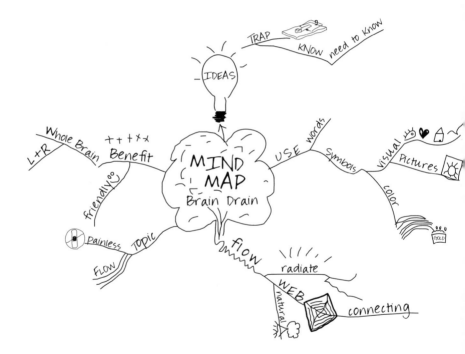

Try One of Your Own

Forced Connections

Forcing anything and everything
to become an UNLIKELY EXPERT

Forced connections is a process of taking any random person, place or thing

that comes to mind (be it living or dead, famous or not) and asking yourself,

"What does this person, place or thing tell me about the issue I'm working on?"

Let's try a forced connections warm-up:

What do a cat and a refrigerator have in common?
Don't stop until you force out 10 connections!

Now let's practice finding connections to real issues.
Because we're toy inventors, we love using toys and
games as unlikely experts, so let's do some

TOYING AROUND

As always, state your problem or concern. Then open your imaginary
Toy Box and let the toys become your teachers. Take a long look at
each toy, note its unique characteristics, and spend a few moments
thinking about what that toy might be "saying" to you.

Let's try it.

*Imagine that you're grappling with whether you should
stay in your job (which you don't particularly like) or
whether to look for something new
(which is scary and unknown).*

7

Now pick a toy.

Mr. Potato Head™ has lots of parts and pieces that can be interchanged to give him a variety of looks. He might be telling you that, just as he has lots of combinations, you too have lots of talents still untapped that might flourish in another situation.

· On the other hand, you might interpret Mr. Potato Head to mean that you already have all that you need to be happy wherever you are. You might challenge yourself to figure out a way to change elements of your present job in some way, just as Mr. Potato Head changes around his appearance, so that your job becomes bearable — and possibly even enjoyable!

Clue™ could teach us about learning from mistakes. When you guess *"Colonel Mustard* in the *library* with the *wrench,"* and your opponent shows you the **wrench,** you don't just throw down your cards and quit. You note on your scorepad that the weapon *isn't* the wrench, and you credit your turn with having learned an important piece of information. One possible Clue interpretation might be that maybe your job really *isn't* the right fit for you, and, like the adjustable wrench, it may be time to make a change.

7

Toys don't provide automatic answers, but they may provide the clues that allow you to come up with an answer that works for you.

Two people struggling with exactly the same problem may come away with two different messages from Mr. Potato Head or Clue. The important thing is that rummaging through the Toy Box allowed both of those people to come away with an AHA! that might never have surfaced had they stuck with their normal patterns of thinking.

Here are a few more toys and the lessons they may have for us:

The **Yo-Yo** teaches us that the ups and downs of life are both normal and rhythmic.

Monopoly™ encourages us to take risks and maybe even go for Park Place.

The **Slinky**™ tells us to be flexible and stretch ourselves just a little farther than we think we can reach.

The **Ouija Board** urges us to trust our intuition.

Rubik's Cube™ demonstrates that persistence pays off.

A **Kaleidoscope** shows us how to change, even slightly, the way we look at a situation, and thus to come up with a whole new picture.

Bubbles encourage us to follow our dreams.

❼

The world of reality has limits; the world of
imagination is boundless.
—*Jean-Jacques Rousseau*

But don't stop with these. Every toy can become a mentor. What was your favorite toy or
game as a child? How could it help
you take a new look at the
situations of your adult life?

Toying Around is not just for
kids, but for anyone who
wants a new spin on looking at
the **Game of Life!**™

7

Click Cards

Click Cards are easy to make and simple to use. They allow you to be a matchmaker and arrange an endless amount of marriages, one of which may become just the solution — or CLICK! — that you're looking for.

Click Cards are Maria's favorite technique, and here's how she uses them.

1.

Fact-find. On each card write down something you *already know* about the problem or issue you're working on.

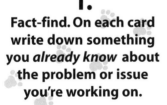

7

2.

Boil these "facts" down to single words or very short phrases. Go for 15-20.

Work-related example: getting ideas for new toys.

Here is a sample of some Click Cards I use when I'm trying to come up with toy ideas. These are all tried-and-true features of previously successful toys. These are all things I know.

For Boys	Try-Me Package	For Girls
Bubbles	Scented	Doll
Role Play	Light	Secret Places
Plush	Gross & Yucky	Soft
Flying	Tub	Action

7

Personal-life example: getting ideas for my master's degree.

When I was trying to choose which areas I wanted to focus on in my flexible master's degree program, I came up with these cards. All the words represent things that either I love to do, or are important to me.

Toy Biz	Kids/ Family	Nature
Close Commute	Teaching	Make a Difference
French	Health/ Fitness	Travel
Computer Skills	Publishing	Organize/ Simplify
Creativity	Self-Employed	Writing

7

3.

Now take small blank cards and write one fact per card. (I use 3" x 5" index cards cut in half.)

4.

When you're ready, spread all the cards face down on a table and mix them. Pick any two at random and see if something CLICKS for you.

Example using my toy Click Cards:

Bubbles + Light
What if there were a bubble toy that lit up? Bubble flashlight? Light-up bubble pipe?

Doll + Secret Places
What if there were a doll whose clothing had all sorts of unexpected hiding places where little girls could keep small treasures?

Example using my personal life Click Cards:

Creativity + Writing
What if I focused on preparing a book or magazine article about what I've learned along the way regarding creativity?

Close Commute + French
What if I designed French classes for adult beginners and taught them in my home?

An alternative way to use Click Cards is to choose *one* card as the base card, and match it — *and only it* — to every other card.

Example using my toy Click Cards: I chose the card that says BALL as my base card:

Ball + Gross-and-Yucky
What about a ball that popped gross things out of it?

Ball + Light
What about a ball that lit up when you bounced it?

Ball + Soft
What about a safe, soft ball? Maybe this is how the NERF™ ball was invented!

7

Example using my personal life Click Cards: I chose CREATIVITY as the base card.

Creativity + Teaching
How about designing a community education course on creativity?

Creativity + Nature
What if I studied the relationship between creativity and various elements of nature?

Creativity + Publishing
What if I wrote a book on inventive creativity?

Get the idea?

Some of the marriages will make more sense than others. Some will be outrageous or funny. Some will be sensible but no particular CLICK will come. Some will produce head-slapping AHAs, and you'll wonder why you didn't think of them sooner. Those are the ones you're looking for.

*Go for it! You may be just a **CLICK** away from solving a problem that's been bugging you for months.*

· · · · ·

Click Cards in a Nutshell

- Identify the challenge.
- Select words or phrases about the key facts.
- Write them on cards.
- Pick any two cards at random.
- Look for connections between the cards picked.
- Push yourself to find as many clicks as you can.

7

Breaking ASSUMPTIONS

Wasn't it a high school coach or teacher who reminded us that "to assume makes an A-S-S out of U and M-E? "

In fact, the ability to identify and challenge assumptions is an admirable quality of creative people. AND, breaking assumptions by asking "**What if** this weren't so?" is a great technique for coming up with exceptional ideas and solutions.

Henry Ford challenged the widely held assumption that the workers had to move to the materials by asking "**What if** we *brought the materials to the workers*?" Voila: the birth of the assembly line!

In the world of toy inventing there have been some wonderful assumption-bashing successes. Here are five of them:

Assumption #1: People don't like to be asked to draw.
Assumption #2: "Q and A" is no fun. It's too much like school.
Assumption #3: Dolls have to be beautiful and lovely.
Assumption #4: Mom will never allow balls to be thrown in the house.
Assumption #5: Boys don't play with dolls.

The first one led to the creation of *Pictionary*™, a game that actually favors people who can't draw. While the true artists busy themselves with shading and perspective, the artistically-challenged win with their stick figure creations! The second assumption resulted in *Trivial Pursuit*™, a game that made both general and specific knowledge fast-paced and fun. *Cabbage Patch*™ dolls broke the third assumption. Their homeliness actually "called to" the hearts and wallets of the consumer. The *Nerf*™ Ball's soft and safe material was the answer to all of Mom's concerns about the fourth assumption. And finally, boys DO play with dolls! Of course, many of you virile types call *GI Joe*™ an "action figure." Please! How different—really—is Joe's Uzi gun and his combat boots from *Barbie*™'s pink purses and high heels! You're busted, macho men!

In our training business, we use this technique regularly to elicit inventive ideas. First we ask participants to list their assumptions about their challenge. Once done, the fun and functional solutions flow easily as they break those assumptions by asking "**What if?**"

Assumptions in a Nutshell

- List all the assumptions you've made about your challenge.
- One by one, ask "**What if** the assumption weren't true, then what could be?"

Fairy Tales

Another simple group technique, guaranteed to involve everyone, is what we call **Fairy Tales.** The academics call it Brain Writing.

Remember a game you played around a bonfire or at a slumber party where one person started a story, was cut off at random, and the next person picked up from the stopping point and went on with the story? The process continued, and you could always depend on hearing some pretty interesting and often bizarre sagas!

7

Borrow this childhood pastime and apply it to your next idea-generating session. Here's how it works:

Start with a clear explanation of the problem, followed by a simple statement of the question. For example:

Problem: People are coming late to work.
Question: How can we get everyone to come on time?

Put blank paper on each table — one or two sheets **more** than the number of people at that table. Write the question on the top of each piece. If you wish, you can also add a few possible solutions to start the ball rolling. Place the pages face down in the middle of the table.

7

Each person takes a paper and adds a suggestion that addresses the question — just a sentence or two will do. When finished, he or she returns the paper to the middle and takes another sheet at random. Always read what was already written and then add your idea. Don't be afraid to piggyback on what went before.

When most of the papers seem full or close to it, ask for volunteers to read some or all of the papers, depending on the size of the group. You'll be surprised at the quantity and quality of the suggestions.

Variation #1

You might have fun adding this feature, especially if the tables have larger groups. Put the "official question" on *most* of the sheets, but *reserve* two or three for completely random "starters" like *Things You Should Never Say to a Nun* or *Once upon a time, a frog hopped onto the road only to find…* This forces people to move back and forth between the silly (nuns and frogs) and the serious (work-related issue), while keeping the brain active and alert.

Variation #2

Place one or more sheets displaying the question in a common area like the lunchroom or copy center. Leave them there to collect ideas for a few days or more, and see what you get. You can use standard-size paper or flip-chart-size sheets taped to the wall with markers nearby.

What makes **Fairy Tales** such a valuable tool is that it provides the protection of anonymity and thereby takes the pressure off people who find it difficult to speak up during a more traditional brainstorming meeting.

Fairy Tales in a Nutshell

- Put a challenge (and possibly even a solution or two) on the top of sheets of paper.
- Circulate these pages encouraging folks to read and add to what they see.

7

The GET YOUR BUTT FIRED! Technique

Here's a sure fire way (yes, pun intended!) to get good ideas.

The next time you're stuck trying to come up with a unique solution, just change your point of view and try to generate 6-10 ideas that will get you fired. You read correctly.

We said "fired," *not* "fired up!"

This is how it works. Once you've got your list that's guaranteed to get you kicked out on your backside, take each idea and tone it down by softening some of the edginess that made it so offensive. Think of your radical idea as an onion, and peel back one layer at a time, going only far enough to remove the nasty parts. You will be surprised to find the new and interesting directions that emerge!

A few years ago, we were asked by the Cancervive Foundation of Los Angeles to develop a game for chronically ill children that would be distributed by Pfizer Pharmaceutical in hospitals throughout the United States. The challenge was daunting. We found ourselves stuck trying to find a theme that might showcase the many challenges faced not only by the chronically ill, but also by their families and medical providers. We decided to **get ourselves fired** and began to come up with bizarre situations that actually made fun of chronic illness. Next, we softened the edges and wound up with a most delightful game called Adventure Park, where roller coaster rides addressed the ups and downs of long-term illnesses, a haunted house dealt with fear and other emotions, and the "Dunk-The-Doc" arcade gave players a chance to express their thoughts about life in the world of hospitals and clinics! It turned out to be a great contribution to chronically ill children — and we didn't get fired!

In a more corporate setting, we recently helped an associate use this technique to come up with PR ideas for one of his clients. The outrageous suggestion that the president of the company walk into the local newspaper office wearing only a cardboard box was toned down into the idea of a paper jack-in-the-box giveaway with a picture of the company president popping out to promote the company's growth.

The **GET YOUR BUTT FIRED** technique is a particularly good one for group brainstorming. Everyone loves the vicarious experience of getting booted for coming up with an outrageous idea, and it really encourages the mildest of personalities to come up with the wildest of ideas.

Try it sometime — alone or with others. Whether or not you come up with the perfect mousetrap for the Acme Extermination Company, we guarantee you'll enjoy being a little bit bad and a little bit playful while

turning the WaCky *into the* workable!

⑦

Get Your Butt Fired! In a Nutshell:

- Develop 6-10 outrageous get-yourself-fired ideas.
- Tone them down until you have a workable solution.

No matter what your age or your life
path … it is not too late or too egotistical
or too selfish or too silly to work on
your creativity.
— *Julia Cameron*

The imagination needs
noodling — long,
inefficient, happy idling,
dawdling and puttering.
— *Brenda Ueland*

I dwell in possibility.
— *Emily Dickinson*

Things To Do or See

- Taking time for your creative spirit
- Mind-expanding field trips
- Books to read and movies to see
- Toys and games to stretch the mind

Things To Do or See

Taking time for your creative spirit

Julia Cameron (author of *The Artist's Way*), Thomas Edison, Wolfgang Amadeus Mozart, AND Charlie and Maria Girsch all encourage time away from the fray as a way to grow in your creative abilities. Earlier, we mentioned Julia Cameron's suggestions for *artists' dates* — a couple of hours set aside weekly to enjoy or explore a new or favored pastime. Maria and Charlie take *field trips* to explore and stimulate their muses.

Always leave enough time in your life to do something that makes you happy, satisfied or even joyous. That has more of an effect on well-being than any other single factor.
— *Paul Hawken*

8

ison was known for taking what we now call *power naps* (Charlie loves these) in the middle of his laboratory, and for fishing *without* bait near his Florida home because he intuitively understood the importance of "sitting a spell" as very important to his creative process.

Mozart wrote in his diaries about the importance of very long walks when he was struggling with one of his musical pieces. It was not unusual for him to "see" a whole piece during his special strolls that often went for miles and miles.

When Maria feels an idea coming on, she immediately draws a hot **bath** for soaking and ruminating. The creative spirit needs time for incubation and stimulation.

Things To Do or See

Mind-expanding field trips

Here are some suggested places to go to refresh your creative spirit:

Visit or browse through any of the following ...
- a shop that sells novelties and collectibles
- a gift or stationery shop
- a mail-order catalogue of unusual products
- a hardware store
- an antique shop
- a surplus store
- an arboretum, conservatory or florist
- a museum for grown-ups or kids
- a lake or river walking path
- a new ethnic restaurant
- a zoo
- a bookstore — new or used

Things To Do or See

Come up with a few of your own field trips!

. . . .

. . . .

. . . .

. . . .

. . . .

. . . .

. . . .

. . . .

. . . .

. . . .

Things To Do or See

Books to read & movies to see

Charlie and Maria's top picks:

BOOKS

The Artist's Way
by Julia Cameron
A marvelous 12-week course for releasing the artist within. You are led to realize your creative self and given lots of straightforward assistance to release and care for that energy.

Creativity
by Mihaly Csikszentmihalyi
A conversation about creative thinking comprised of interviews with contemporary men and women who have been honored for breakthrough achievements in their domain. Rich in stories and insight.

Things To Do or See

Orbiting the Giant Hairball
by Gordon McKenzie
A delightful look at the efforts and antics of a creative person in a large corporation. Gordon tells stories about himself and his employer in a wonderfully attractive compendium of anecdotes. This book is for anyone trying to ignite his or her creative spirit — or just keep it alive and well.

Thinkertoys
by Michael Michalko
A great handbook of tools and techniques to push your brainstorming from every possible direction. His thoughtful explanations of each approach are followed by a simple blueprint for using the technique.

How To Think Like Leonardo DaVinci
by Michael Gelb
Seven principles of DaVincian creativity. This book is fun to read and its graphics will take you on an all-expense paid trip to ancient Italy. (Maria's all-time favorite book!)

Things To Do or See

Creative Problem Solving and Opportunity Finding
by J. Daniel Couger

Though often used as a college textbook, this collection of creative techniques is very un-college-textbook-like. An unusual combination of both reference and relaxation, with fun graphics to boot!

What a Great Idea!
by Chic Thompson

This feels like a casual, after-dinner conversation with an old friend about creativity. Easy to read and easy to digest.

The Creative Spirit
by Daniel Goleman

Based on a PBS miniseries, this comprehensive exploration of creativity and the creative process is a visual treat, chock full of great information.

en Soup
y Laurence G. Boldt
you like quotes, this book, sub-
tled *Tasty Morsels of Wisdom*
om Great Minds East & West,
ontains wise words that will
arm your creative spirit.

Five-Star Mind
by Tom Wujec
The "McMedley" of creativity.
Short, to-the-point exercises and
activities to stimulate the brain, as
well as spark creative potential.

Things To Do or See

Other recommendations:

. . . .

. . . .

. . . .

. . . .

. . . .

. . . .

. . . .

. . . .

. . . .

. . . .

. . . .

. . . .

Things To Do or See

MOVIES

Defending Your Life
with Albert Brooks
A delightful look at the power of fear as a
block to living and creativity.

Life Is Beautiful
with Roberto Benigni
The power of imagination as a tool for
creating a better life than the one you are in.

8

Things To Do or See

Phenomenon
with John Travolta
Explores the power and potential of the
mind as a gateway to creative genius.

Patch Adams
with Robin Williams
Celebrates the healing power of humor.

Amélie
with Audrey Tautou
Recall your own
imaginative and curious
childhood when you
watch the opening credits.
Also, be warned that this
movie could cause
terminal playfulness.

Things To Do or See

Other recommendations:

. . . .

. . . .

. . . .

. . . .

. . . .

. . . .

. . . .

. . . .

. . . .

. . . .

8

Things To Do or See

Toys & games to stretch the mind

Legos™ • Toobers & Zots™

(or any construction set). Put a bucket of these build-
ing toys out on the table and kids of all ages find themselves exploring, imagining and expressing.

Clay • PlayDoh™

(or any sculpting material). These are flexible,
tactile and satisfying compounds. Everyone becomes
a Michelangelo when busy hands shape endless
forms, each iteration different! Remember to expend
your energy on imagination, not judgment.

Things To Do or See

Clue™ • Mindtrap™ • Set™

(and the daily puzzles in the newspaper). These are all puzzle formulas with different degrees of difficulty, and they provide lots of opportunities to exercise your deductive powers. Keep in mind that they don't always have to be a competition. Answering questions can be a collaborative effort as you learn to rely on each other's strengths. The family room, coffee table, kitchen counter or bathroom are good places to keep a pack of cards from any mind-stretching game..

Catch Phrase™ • Pictionary™ • Charades

(and any improvisation games). These provide excellent opportunities to "let go" and experience the "yes, and..." energy of your childhood play. The challenge is thinking on your feet, and using whatever comes to mind to communicate the essence of the message. These often result in plenty of laughter, which means lots of endorphins will be flowing!

8

BrainQuest™ • TriBond™ • Outburst™

(or any trivia-type games). These information-based games are all about remembering and associating trivia stored somewhere in your brain. The important thing here is to avoid judging your "performance." These are also great for the bathroom and provide plenty of opportunities to learn on the go! (Groan.)

Finger Painting • Water Color

Klutz Press sells a particularly user-friendly watercolor book that we highly recommend. Both of these art forms are inexpensive ways to experience the challenge of mixing colors and the satisfaction of filling page after page with your mind's doodles.

Odyssey of the Mind™ • Destination Imagination™

These organized groups, often based in schools, are a great venue for children to keep in touch with their innate creativity and for adults to remember and utilize theirs as they support or coach creativity teams.

8

Things To Do or See

Your own toy & game suggestions

_____

_____

_____

_____

_____

_____

_____

_____

_____

_____

8

Things To Do or See

Seven Practices of Inventivity

- The Seven Practices of the "Inventive Creative"
- Permission Slip
- The Rest

Seven Practices of Inventivity

We're at the end of the tour, but there are no badges to turn in. In fact, you'll soon be given something to take away with you.

Whether you've read snippets of this book when the spirit moved you, or the whole book from cover to cover, you've been exposed to a large body of information. One of the fundamental processes of creative thinking is **diverge-first-and-then-converge.**
Diverging means throwing out lots of possibilities. We have done that in the previous chapters by sharing with you a variety of tools and techniques, habits and qualities, personal insights and under-standings. Now we would like to **converge,** that is, to compress it all into a simple sum-mary. Charlie says it best in a short talk he is often requested to give. He calls it:

The Seven Practices of the Inventive Creative.

The Seven Practices of The "Inventive Creative"

Everyday Things That Absolutely Anybody Can Do To Stimulate Creativity

Dream dreams.

Einstein has reminded us of the power of imagination and we have encouraged you to practice stretching yourself, especially in your head, so that you're ready to take a creative risk when the opportunity arises. We've talked of Alice in Wonderland and the Queen's practice of having six impossible ideas before breakfast to encourage you to start imagining "impossible inventions" of your own.

Row, row, row your boat,
Gently down the stream.
Merrily, merrily, merrily, merrily,
Life is but a dream. ....

Being a dreamer and schemer prepares you to adopt our **What If? What Else? Why Not?** mantra. Another way to say this is

Dream
Dare
Do

and it all starts with the willingness to visualize some new possibility. A Dell™ computer ad once promised, "If you can imagine it, we can build it." Those who practice dreaming will be astonished by the power of imagined possibility and will always find themselves ready to take a creative risk or leap.

Be open and prepared.

Louis Pasteur said that "Luck favors a prepared mind," and it's easy to stay prepared if you're always looking ahead to some new possibility, going to new places, trying some new widget, or seeking some new interest. Creative people love to know and experience more. They never stop learning and continually find stimulating opportunities to enliven their spirit and their thinking. They look at life as if through a kaleidoscope, always willing to turn it a bit to get a new perspective from a different point of view.

Seven Practices of Inventivity

The Boy Scouts encourage us to **Be Prepared!** Julia Cameron's "artist's dates" and our own "field trips" are perfect examples of staying prepared. Even though we are toy inventors, our field trips are not always business-related. Of course, we routinely wander through toy departments, but we're just as comfortable visiting a hardware store, a museum exhibit, a holiday parade or the animal barns at the State Fair.

One never knows where inspiration will come from. It is said that Henry Ford got the idea for mass production from watching meat packers. The idea for a wood-activity concept that we sold came from a *Better Homes & Gardens* article, and the inspiration for an outdoor-activity item came from watching a municipal worker paint stripes in a parking lot. No place is too far-out for an "inventive creative" to discover insight or wisdom!

Life is a daring adventure or nothing.
— *Helen Keller*

Try new and different things.

This will help get you out of the rut into which even the best habits can trap you. Creative people enjoy the energy that comes from stepping out of their comfort zone. They are willing to take risks and improvise when originality is called for. They knock down the blocks that habit and fear present so as to arrive at a new place, ready and eager to embrace the challenge.

Explore something different every day. Try a new recipe. Read a new point of view. Listen to an unfamiliar song. Sing or dance. Take a long, quiet walk. Hug a friend. Wave to the kids on the school bus.
— *Margie Lapanja*

By now you should believe that you definitely have creative potential and that you can get your creative juices going by regularly using our (or your own) stretch-ercises to enliven your brain. Many of the tools and techniques we've included are examples of new and different things you can try.

> Life is so scary, it's not even worth worrying about.
> — *Gertrude Stein*

We've also called out some blocks to creativity, and now it's up to you to acknowledge them, but then keep on going. If you are willing to stretch and try the new and different, you will free your creative spirit and no longer be paralyzed by fear. You will be able to reinvent yourself, your life and your career.

Find quiet time.

4

Mozart took his long walks and Edison napped right in his lab with pencil and paper nearby. Great minds know the importance of taking time away from the fray. They stop "doing," and just let themselves "be" for a while.

The subconscious needs quiet time for the power of incubation to be effective. Think of how "slow cooking" releases the juices stored in the mix of ingredients in a pot of soup or stew. Keep this image in mind and you will begin to see the power of taking yourself out of the daily fracas long enough to let your own creative juices simmer.

There are so many ways to enjoy the effects of quiet times. **Walks** gave Mozart time to be alone with his confusion, and they can do the same for you. Edison discovered what today is called the **power nap.** He frequently got his ideas on his way into and out of sleep. Others have turned to **journaling** as a way to process life and gain insight. Some proclaim the quieting power of **meditation** as a source of inspiration. **Contemplation** gets high marks for developing an awareness of nature and beauty.

There are endless ways to "get quiet." Find one that works for you and enjoy the gift of centering and calming — and be sure to keep your idea-trapping utensils handy. If you're taking the time to invoke your creative spirit, why not capture the gifts as they come?

Make mistakes.

5

As inventors we have a built-in opportunity to make mistakes. Prototyping! It actually becomes a time when our hands and the materials we're working with conspire to let us know where we can't go, but more excitingly, where we can! It's an interesting process and always one full of learning.

Making mistakes relates to the "Why Not?" of our mantra. We have found that the sooner we try, the sooner we will learn from our mistakes, and, more importantly, we find out what the materials will allow us to do. Recently, while working on a special perfume-making-toy, we had the experience of discovering "by mistake" a simple and magical way of powering our fragrance factory. Mattel ended up purchasing the rights to this happy mistake discovered in the late hours and after multiple attempts. We hope that many children will enjoy the fruits of this *felix culpa*.

If you build it, they will come. ...
— *Field of Dreams*

Share the dream.

Our experience tells us that something special happens when you voice your "What ifs?" to friendly and receptive ears.

Sharing your dreams actually accomplishes two things. First, there's power in acknowledging your ideas. They become real and therefore have a better chance of escaping the paralyzing block of fear that could keep them from ever seeing the light of day. Secondly, you often develop support from your friends and listeners in these moments of vulnerable sharing. We've all had the experience of telling friends that we are thinking of planning a trip somewhere — only to receive lots of suggestions on how to get there, where to stay and what to see. We are collaborators at heart and, given the opportunity, we will jump to the aid of any fellow traveler chasing a creative possibility.

What if I went to:

Europe?

The beach?

The mountains?

Let go and trust.

There's nothing worse than people with one, single, self-absorbing idea. They can get so completely obsessed with their concept that they miss the opportunity to collaborate in order to "build that better mousetrap." One of our greatest collaborators, Peter Pook, was capable of coming up with endless ideas. Yet he instinctively knew how to detach and let go of his own ego involvement so he could cooperate with others to massage the idea until it was both fun and viable. He is one of the best idea-generators that we ever worked with.

Letting go and trusting are really about detaching from an expected result in order to let your "baby" go and take on a life of its own. The benefit is that

you will be fun to work with.

You will come to trust that your ideas will discover their own identities as they enjoy the collaborative support of your team and associates. Best of all, you will be left with the energy to develop yet another idea or to support other people in achieving theirs.

Now it's your turn to act.

Fill out the following Permission Slip and detach it. Keep it in your wallet, your purse, on the corner of your mirror, or anywhere you are likely to see it — reminding yourself of these 7 Practices.

Inventivity
Permission Slip

_____
your name here

has permission to:

Dream Dreams
Be Open and Prepared
Try New & Different Things
Find Quiet Time
Have Fun & Make Mistakes
Share the Dream
Let Go and Trust

_____
date

Inventivity Permission Slip

Seven Practices of Inventivity

Some closing thoughts, if we may… It bears reminding that **Inventivity is an inside job!** You have the ability to create — in your own words and in your own way — but that potential won't flourish unless and until you are willing to become intentional about your efforts. In these pages we have tried to simplify the path to **inventive creativity** by providing exercises that are truly do-able on a daily basis. The rest is up to you.

Once you have begun your journey, you too will experience a certain satisfaction that Mary Richards talks about in one of our favorite quotes. You will find in her words the promise of a serenity that can only be achieved in the discovery and execution of an uncommonly creative answer to life's challenges.

> We have to believe that a creative being lives within ourselves whether we like it or not, and that we must get out of its way, for it will give us no peace until we do.
>
> — *Mary Richards*

The Reach of Creativity Central

Services We teach, train,
facilitate and speak.

Occasions Conference keynotes and breakouts,
meetings, workshops, seminars,
brainstorming sessions, retreats, and
distance learning programs.

Clients We love impressing you with our major corporate clients
like Target, 3M, Northwest Airlines, Pillsbury, General Mills,
Fortis Insurance, and the St. Paul
Companies to name a few. But
we also have served tens of
thousands of people in smaller
organizations, educational
institutions and non-profits,
helping them to discover or
increase their creative potential.

*People are people, and creativity is a timeless topic in both work and everyday life.
If we can help you, please contact us via our website.*

What You Can Look For From Creativity Central

Our Topic and Style

- Creativity for everyone, every day, everywhere
- Presented in an interactive, edu-taining way
- Where everyone leaves with tools they can start trying immediately

Our Guarantee

We offer a money-back guarantee that says "Participants will leave our presentation inspired and motivated by their own creativity, or you get your money back!"

On our website, you can find lots of good reasons why we unabashedly offer this guarantee. You can also find a regularly updated list of our clients.

Our Products

On our website, we offer a variety of products for sale. In addition to this book, they include Creativity À La Card (a classic and classy deck of powerful quotes, each with an appropriate Stretch-ercise™), mousepads, Think Pen™, hats, and popoids. We even have some items that are free for the downloading. Log onto www.creativitycentral.com.

Our Custom Cover Books

Many companies have ordered copies of *Fanning the Creative Spirit* with their logo on the front cover, as well as a special introduction, to use as gifts and/or training tools for their employees and customers. View some of these custom covers on our website to see if they make sense for your company.

IDEA SWAT TEAMS

Physicist-philosopher Freeman T. Dyson observes that technology and innovation are used mainly for profit. Why not, he suggests, use these creative energies and systems to serve social needs as well?

Touched by his challenge, we helped develop **IDEA SWAT TEAMS.** These are pro-bono sessions offered to groups whose focus is on social benefit rather than economic profit. Here's how they work. The group identifies their challenge. We facilitate and often invite additional outside creatives to mix with their "key players." The end result is a stewpot of innovative ideas that the group can use as they please.

Some of our IDEA SWAT TEAM beneficiaries are the Ronald McDonald House, Make-A-Wish Minnesota, the Compas Community Arts Program, and the Governor's Council on Developmental Disabilities.

We encourage you to steal this concept and organize similar events for the benefit of your own commuity.

CHEERS TO YOUR UNCORKED CREATIVE SPIRIT!

What did you like in this book?

_____

_____

_____

_____

_____

_____

_____

_____

How will you use it?

_____

_____

_____

_____

We would love to hear about any ahas or insights you have experienced.
Please contact us via our website at **www.creativitycentral.com**.

Warning: These pages could prove helpful in leading you on a path of *creative* thinking and doing.

is good to have an end to journey toward, but it is the journey that matters in the end.

— *Ursula K. LeGuin*

The End.
The Beginning …

Creativity
Central

For a daily stretch-ercise or more information on
what we offer and how we can work with you,
check out our Web site:

www.creativitycentral.com

book design by

www.avenuebdesign.com